Er

My friend Terri LaPoint is a tireless warrior for FREEDOM. She pioneered journalistic investigations of "medical kidnappings" at a time when lamestream media ignored the families crying out for justice. Her passion for truth is tenacious. *Voices That Will Not Be Silenced* is riveting and eye-opening. In this book, Terri connects dots few have dared investigate, but which we must face if we are to stop the rampant trafficking of children right here in America.

Not only does this book expose wrong-doing, it offers hope to parents who are fighting for their children. It is important that we hear the voices of those who can no longer speak for themselves, and that we work together to make a difference.

Dr. Gina Loudon
National TV Talk Show Host,
bestselling author, and mother of five

The untold history of America is the victimization of our children by our own government. Over the decades this has taken on many forms; institutionalization, mandated vaccines, slave trade, child labor, and child trafficking, much of it driven by leaders and lawmakers who have passed laws and directed tax dollars to privately run organizations.

For half a century, lawmakers have monetized children through federal programs, including education, healthcare management, and child welfare. The tragedy is that child welfare funding is not just about putting a dollar sign on the head of every child, it is about how they do it. For child welfare, state agencies gain federal funds by stripping children from their home of origin: their parents, their grandparents, and all extended family members.

A few lawmakers have seen the problem and attempted to initiate changes. Arkansas' State Senator Linda Collins was one of them. Senator Collins listened to Kathy Hall's tragic story on the loss of her daughter and granddaughter, and started her own investigation into the financial corruption behind Arkansas' Department of Children and Families Services (DCFS). The result was tragic for both.

The only way the system will change is with public awareness and public outrage. This book is a step towards this goal. I want to personally thank Terri LaPoint and Kathy Hall working so hard to preserve the truth.

Connie Reguli
Attorney and Family Advocate
Founder of Family Forward Project

When I first met Terri LaPoint, she was a voice for midwives and homeschoolers. Later, when she learned that children and senior citizens were being seized from their families, she jumped in to investigate their stories and learn the facts. It has never been about an agenda for her. It is about what is right.

In *Voices That Will Not Be Silenced*, she tells a story that could just as easily happen to your family or mine. Senator Linda Collins-Smith (AK) was a warrior for Angel moms like Kathy Hall as well as many other families fighting for their children. Through this book, we can hear her passionate voice for justice. If we will hear the message of this book, we can continue her legacy and make the future better for all of our children.

Sen. John Loudon (R-MO, Ret.)
Philanthropist, business owner, and father of five

Voices That Will Not Be Silenced is a story which needs to be told in all its appalling and horrific and heartbreaking details, coupled with the courage of the champions for their own children and others. Terri LaPoint is an excellent writer. I almost became a speed reader trying to find out what was going to happen next.

This important book includes the record of two compassionate and courageous ladies who gave their lives to protect innocent children and expose their abusers. Sen. Nancy Schaeffer was my friend and a role model. May their sacrifice inspire and instruct others to step into the gap to stop the carnage.

Eunie Smith, President
Eagle Forum of Alabama
Leading the pro-family movement since 1972

Nationwide our hospitals use Social Workers and the Judicial system to legally kidnap children with genetic disorders needed for medical and pharmaceutical research. Since 1997, Title IV foster care funding has created financial windfalls for the politicians who use our children to balance state budgets. It takes someone courageous to investigate and expose these crimes that represent hundreds of millions of dollars yearly.

Terri LaPoint has dedicated her life to researching and publishing these stories. It has been my honor to work alongside her and many other brave family Advocates seeking justice, working to reunite the families ripped apart by false allegations and changing the laws that protect the kidnappers.

The families within this book are Heroes deserving badges of courage and medals of honor. Their service to this country is represented by their own flesh and blood being stolen away and sold for profit. Their stories deserve to be heard and Terri has sacrificed so that you, the reader... could know the truth.

Sherrie Saunders
Appointed Parent Advocate to the Alabama
Council of Developmental Disability,
and Mother to a child with a rare genetic disorder

Congratulations on taking your first step in becoming a voice for those whose voices cannot be heard!

Voices That Will Not Be Silenced is a not just a call to action in the areas of injustice addressed in this book, but in the call to shine a light on all acts of injustice and every work of darkness in our day.

Like a modern-day Esther, Terri's unwavering commitment to "not be silent" as she has stood up and spoken out on every level of influence addressing these overlooked atrocities when so many have chosen to simply look away is not only an inspiring read, but also a manifesto of courage and a practical manual for how to address the present evils of our day.

Terri's insight, understanding, and advocacy for the voiceless victims of medical kidnapping and unjustly separated families has been a Godsend in creating grassroots awareness, pioneering legislation on the national level to bring about lasting change while practically educating so many on a local level.

It has been said, *"The only thing necessary for the triumph of evil is for good men (and women) to do nothing."* The evils of our day have lurked in the shadows for far too long and while no one can do everything, everyone can do something to shine a light on these works of darkness as together we turn this tide.

Are you ready to make a difference? If so, ***this is the book for you!***

Pastor Jason Hooper
Senior Pastor of King's Way Church
President & Founder of King's Way College

VOICES
THAT WILL NOT BE
SILENCED

Terri LaPoint

Voices That Will Not Be Silenced
Copyright © 2024 by Terri LaPoint

All Rights Reserved.
No part of this book may be reproduced, stored in a retrieval system, or transmitted, in any manner whatsoever without written permission from the publisher, except in the case of brief quotations embodied in news articles, reviews, or informational posts.

Publisher's Note: The information in this book is for educational and general informational purposes only. While every attempt has been made to verify information provided in this book, the author assumes no responsibility for any errors, inaccuracies, or omissions. If advice concerning legal matters is needed, the services of a qualified professional should be sought. This book is not intended for use as a source of legal advice.

Scripture quotations marked TPT are taken from The Passion Translation®, Copyright © 2017, 2018, 2020 by Passion & Fire Ministries, Inc. Used by permission. All rights reserved. ThePassionTranslation.com. Scripture quotations marked NIV are taken from THE HOLY BIBLE: NEW INTERNATIONAL VERSION®, 1973, 1978, 1984, 2011 International Bible Society. Used by permission of Zondervan. All rights reserved. Scripture quotations marked NKJV are taken from the New King James Version. Copyright © 1982 by Thomas Nelson, Inc. Used by permission. All rights reserved. Scripture quotations marked KJV are taken from the King James Version. Scripture quotations marked AMP are taken from the Amplified® Bible. Copyright © 2015 by The Lockman Foundation, La Habra, CA 90631. Used by permission. All rights reserved. Scripture quotation marked NASB are taken from the New American Standard Bible®, Copyright © 1960, 1971, 1977, 1995, 2020 by The Lockman Foundation. All rights reserved.

Unless otherwise noted, photos ©Kathy Hall. Used by permission.
Back cover author photo copyright ©Shara Michelle, Freedom Public Press

ISBN 13: 979-8-218-39743-2
Printed in the United States of America
www.RealNewsSpark.com

RealNewsSpark.com
"Real news that sparks people to make a difference"

VOICES THAT WILL NOT BE SILENCED

Terri LaPoint

Dedication

To every parent, grandparent, and relative fighting for the restoration of your family.

To every family member mourning the loss of one stolen from you.

To every child unjustly taken from your loving family.

To my dear friend Mary B. who faithfully prayed and encouraged me through the writing of this book. Before the book was published, she left us to join the great cloud of witnesses in the heavenly realm. I know she is now cheering on those here on earth who are fighting for their family. Mary was a mother of many and a champion of families in this life; I know she remains so in the next.

Isaiah 42:22-23 (NIV)

But this is a people plundered and looted,

all of them trapped in pits

or hidden away in prisons.

They have become plunder,

with no one to rescue them;

they have been made loot,

with no one to say, "Send them back."

[or "Restore."]

23 Which of you will listen to this

or pay close attention in time to come?

Contents

Preface 12

1 - Different from the Others 15
2 - A Knock on the Door 19
3 - Big Misunderstanding, Right? 27
4 - It's Not Supposed to Work This Way 34
5 - Downward Spiral 42
6 - Sirens, and More Sirens 51
7 - Hailey 59
8 - David 65
9 - Fighting for Justice 74
10 - Where is Justice? 82
11 - Soulless Eyes 87
12 - "No Escape from This Nightmare" 92
13 - "You Have Help Now" 98
14 - Secrets 105
15 - Never Forgotten 113
16 - Little Rock 115
17 - Family Forward Project 123
18 - Scars and Fears 128
19 - She Had it All Along 132
20 - Angel Families 136
21 - Adventures in DC 145
22 - No Slowing Down 154
23 - "Nobody's Looking for These Kids" 163
24 - A Right Way and a Wrong Way 167

25 - Followed 175
26 - "He's Going to Kill Me" 179
27 - Something's Wrong... 185
28 - Kill Switch 192
29 - "We Got You" 201
30 - "Did I Fall Down a Rabbit Hole?" 207
31 - Trafficking and Fraud 215
32 - Twists and Turns, and an Explosion 223
33 - Hear Their Voices 231
Appendix 1 ~ God's Heart for Families 238
Appendix 2 ~ Senator Nancy Schaefer........................... 242
Appendix 3 ~ Guardianship Abuse 251
Citations and End Notes 258

Preface

I met Kathy Hall for the first time in September of 2019. A mutual friend realized Kathy and I were both in Washington, D.C., at the same time. She insisted I meet with her and hear her story.

A few phone calls and an Uber ride later, I sat down with the petite grandmother with fire in her eyes as she shared a tiny portion of her story with me. There were similarities, to be sure, between her story and any of the hundreds I had investigated and reported for the online news source MedicalKidnap.com. But there was so much more. She was also an Angel Mom—the parent of a child killed by someone in the country illegally.

Through Kathy's journey, she became close friends with State Senator Linda Collins (Arkansas) who worked with her, digging into the tragedies that befell Kathy's family. The two worked together to bring attention to the plight of Angel Families and families dealing with Child Protective Services, until the abrupt end to their relationship four months before Kathy's trip to D.C.

A couple months after Kathy and I met, we were again in D.C., this time both of us joining advocates with Family Forward Project—a grassroots group of grandmothers and parents who help families and educate lawmakers regarding issues involving foster care and Child Protective Services (CPS) The more time I spent with Kathy, I knew there was something very special about her. She asked me to write her story, but by the end of this trip, I knew this was much bigger than a single article, or even a series of articles. I asked her, "How much of your story do you want me to tell?"

Her eyes fixed on mine with steely determination. "All of it."

At that moment I sensed Holy Spirit telling me that this—Kathy Hall's story—was the book God wanted me to write, and I said, "This is a book, not a few articles. Yes. I'll do it."

What you hold in your hands is the result of four years of research, interviews, prayers, and tears. It is the story of Kathy's daughter, her granddaughter, and her best friend, from Kathy's unique perspective. It is not my story. It is theirs.

Much darkness is being exposed in our world, from Epstein's island to child trafficking. Children go missing at the border—that is something most people, by now, know about. But what about the children within our own borders? Before I met Kathy, I remember reading a statement from the U.S. Department of Justice which stated that the largest supplier of children for the child sex trafficking industry in the United States was the foster care system. I can never forget those words.

What was Senator Collins investigating? What did she know about before she was stopped from speaking out? And how does what she knew connect with Kathy's story of her granddaughter being taken from her daughter by CPS? This book will answer those questions and more. My hope is that you will hear these voices that will not be silenced, and that their lives will spark a fire in you to get involved and make a difference.

Blessings,
Terri LaPoint - 2023

Note: The primary source for the book is Kathy Hall. Extensive interviews were conducted by the author, followed by diligent research. All texts, posts, tweets, and letters are quoted from the original sources verbatim, without edits of grammar or spelling.

At the time of the events in the book, X was known as Twitter and posts to Twitter were referred to as "tweets." The language in this book reflects the terms as they were known at the time of use.

Some names have been changed to protect the innocent. These are indicated by endnotes.

1 - Different from the Others

"No way!" Kathy Hall had heard it all before, and she was determined not to go down that road again. "It hurts too much."

Sam[1] pleaded with her to give it one more shot. "Please, just give Senator Collins-Smith a call. You really need to talk to her. She wants to speak with you."

Kathy sighed. She explained to Sam that she had already spoken with three Arkansas legislators. "They all listen to what I have to say, and they tell me how sorry they are. But that's the end of it. I don't hear back. I don't think they ever give it a second thought."

Sam could hear the discouragement in his friend's voice over the phone. He also knew Senator Linda Collins-Smith. She was not like most other legislators.

He persisted, "I'm telling you, you need to call her. She asked me to give you her phone number."

"Whatever, Sam. I've heard it all before. It's a waste of time."

Honestly, she thought as she hung up the phone, *I don't have the kind of emotional energy to invest in chasing another rabbit hole that goes nowhere.* Her thoughts turned toward her beautiful daughter Hailey, taken from them too soon in a violent hit-and-run by a man who was in the country illegally. Hailey was only eighteen years old. Tears slipped down her cheeks as she fought back the image of her youngest child's body laying lifeless on the hospital bed, eyes wide open but missing that spark of laughter in them that had always been there for most of her short life.

Kathy shook herself out of her dark thoughts. Dinner was not going to make itself. She took a deep breath, got up from her computer desk, and forced her weary body to the kitchen.

She whispered a prayer for God to watch over her granddaughter Brooklyn, Hailey's little girl. She would be two and a half by now, but no one in the family had seen her since Hailey's death. The Arkansas Department of Human Services (DHS, or Child Protective Services) had seen to that. The injustice of it all was maddening. She never should have been taken from them, and now she was in the hands of strangers.

Several days later, on May 29, 2018, Kathy sat down at her computer to check the news and her Twitter [later rebranded as X] feed on social media. The weight of her grief overwhelmed her and she pounded out her feelings on the keyboard in a Twitter post. She wrote about how hard it was going from day to day missing her daughter and granddaughter. Nothing in life had ever been harder for her than simply facing life each day without them.

To her surprise, Senator Linda Collins-Smith posted a tweet back to her that afternoon:

"Why is this hard? You say you have not had help. You have it now! Here is my cell number 870-[xxx-xxxx]. Who is your State Senator? We can get you an appointment w/the Senators office? It doesn't have to keep going on twitter that gets you nowhere, well it got you to me."

Kathy's first thought held a substantial dose of skepticism, *Sure, you will.*

She read the Senator's post again. Her eyes opened wide and she almost fell out of her chair when she realized the Senator had put her own personal cell phone number in the tweet, publicly, online, for any wacko to see.

She honestly held no hope this Senator would be any different from the others as far as helping her, but Kathy decided she needed to reply, at least to get Linda's phone number off of social media. She quickly composed a direct message, saying, "I take it that you've heard my story, but really you need to take your personal phone number off-line, because you're going to get a lot of weirdos calling, and probably calls throughout the night now by different people."

Linda replied, "Can you call me?"

Kathy hesitated, then dialed the Senator's number, steeling herself to tell her family's story once again to someone who may or may not take her seriously.

They talked for two and a half hours.

Their conversation ended with Linda asking Kathy to give her a couple days to check into her story. "It's not that I don't believe you," she said, "but we have had constituents come in before and tell us their stories. We've gone to bat for them, and then come to find out things were not quite the way they said. I just need to check everything out."

People really need to be honest when they tell their stories, Kathy thought to herself, *because it hurts the rest of us who are being truthful and really need help.* Out loud she said, "I understand. I know my story sounds crazy, and I feel crazy telling people about it."

Linda's response encouraged her. "Nobody could make this stuff up."

Kathy hung up the phone with a glimmer of hope in her heart, the first she'd felt in a long time. Maybe, just maybe, this legislator was different.

That glimmer vanished when, a week later, there was no response from Linda. Not a whisper. Kathy gave in to her original skepticism. *Just like I thought. Another one that makes all the promises and does nothing.*

A couple days later, her phone rang. It was Senator Linda Collins-Smith. Kathy answered to hear apologies from the Senator. "I'm so sorry that I have not gotten back with you, but it has been like pulling teeth just trying to get answers on your case. I looked into everything you told me, and I finally got enough verification."

Linda's voice cracked, and she started crying. "I'm so sorry. I cannot believe this has happened in my state. I cannot believe the stuff I am reading and what I am seeing. I believed you, but I did not—" Linda took a deep breath to compose herself before continuing, "you know, I still had my reservations about whether it was as serious as what you had said."

Her next words sent a chill down Kathy's spine, "Kathy, it's worse than what you told me."

The determination in Linda's voice was unmistakable. "I want to help. I am not going to stop. You know that I just lost my reelection campaign, right? But I am still in office now, and we are going to accomplish as much as possible by the end of my term."

Linda was true to her word. Before long they spoke on the phone almost daily until their conversations came to a screeching halt, through no choice of their own, a year later.

2 - A Knock on the Door

The first time Kathy held her youngest child Hailey Cyell King was in the newborn intensive care unit. She never dreamed she would say goodbye to her only eighteen years later in another ICU.

Hailey was born ten weeks early on November 17, 1997. She had to be rushed to another hospital immediately after birth. The moment Kathy was able to leave the hospital herself, she made a beeline to be with her baby and her husband Tom King at the newborn ICU, where she held her beautiful baby girl for the first time.

From her first breath, Hailey was a fighter with a zest for life.

It was not long before tiny Hailey was able to join the rest of her siblings at home—an older sister and two older brothers. Her prematurity left her with a lifelong hearing loss, which in turn affected her speech, but she never let it slow her down. Her ability to carry a tune was questionable at best; nonetheless, she loved to sing and play the guitar and keyboard.

When her big brothers played baseball, she wanted to play, too. She started playing softball at age five and continued the sport her entire life. Her favorite color was red. She loved tacos and egg rolls.

Life was a joy with Hailey around. She was the "happiest little girl,"[1] according to her mother. No matter what the situation was, Hailey found a reason to laugh. Sometimes she laughed so much her no-nonsense mother would scold her, telling her, "It's not funny. Stop laughing!"

As she grew up, Hailey tried to see the best in everyone. When she was a teenager, kids sometimes made fun of her because of the way she talked. Instead of becoming angry or defensive, the petite blonde laughed with them. When Kathy asked her why, she told her mother she refused to let them see her cry. She would rather make them her friends than let them think their words hurt her.

She had dreams of joining the Navy after graduation, following in the footsteps of her beloved step-father Jeff Hall. He retired from the military after serving twenty-six years in the Navy and Army and received a purple heart during his service in Iraq.

Hailey had just turned sixteen when she found out she was pregnant. She never planned to be a teenage mom, but Hailey embraced the concept of motherhood the same way she did most things in life—with joy and hope. She never entertained any thought of ending her pregnancy or giving up her baby for adoption. She wanted to be a mother, and she knew she had the love and support of her family to help her face whatever challenges parenting her baby would bring.

Meanwhile, Kathy's mother and step-father, Hailey's grand-parents, were experiencing health problems. Her mother begged the family to move closer to their place in Arkansas. When Hailey was six months pregnant, her family loaded up everything and moved from Colorado to a big, beautiful brick home with columns on the front porch. The house was in an upscale neighborhood in northwest Fayetteville, Arkansas, not far from her grandparents' home—a move that would change their lives in ways they could not begin to imagine.

From the very beginning, baby Brooklyn Christine was wanted and welcomed by the entire family. She was born on October 21, 2014, and lived with Hailey and her family. For the first month of Brooklyn's life, Hailey and the baby slept in Kathy and Jeff's room—Brooklyn in her bassinet and Hailey on a futon—because Hailey was afraid she wouldn't hear the baby if she woke up.

They adjusted to life with the new baby, and Hailey went back to school. She also worked part-time at the local Whataburger. While she was in school or at work, Nana Kathy took care of Brooklyn.

When Brooklyn was about five months old, Hailey was diagnosed with postpartum depression, something not uncommon in new mothers and about twice as prevalent in teenage mothers as in older moms. Kathy took her daughter to the hospital to get her help.

To this day, Kathy believes that is what initially put Hailey and Brooklyn on the radar of Arkansas DHS[2]—the Department of Human Services, or Child Protective Services (CPS). She later learned that the hospital reported the postpartum depression to DHS. A social worker spoke with Hailey at the hospital, but they heard nothing more from her after that. Hailey started meeting with a school counselor to help her with her postpartum depression.

Hailey began her senior year of high school in the fall. She had always done well in school, and she was determined to work hard to get caught up on credits so she could graduate on time.

Once, a social worker showed up at her school to talk to her. Hailey told her mother they said they just wanted to make sure she was taking her medication prescribed for postpartum depression. They never went to her house or checked on the baby. Neither she nor her mother though anything of it. *After all, social workers were there to help people*, Kathy believed. *Child Protective Services was all about protecting children from horrible, abusive parents. Surely there was nothing to worry about.*

Hailey had no idea she had found her way into the crosshairs of the system, and she continued on with life, blissfully unaware of the storm brewing for her behind the scenes.

In early November Hailey planned a three-day getaway to visit a cousin in Ohio. Her plan was to take Brooklyn with her, but Kathy suggested she leave the baby at home with her and Jeff since Brooklyn was just getting over a cold. Hailey agreed to let her stay behind, confident her little one was in good hands. She was excited about seeing her cousin, and she shared that excitement with her friends and teachers at school.

Somehow the news she was going out of town reached social workers with the Department of Human Services. Their family's nightmare was about to begin.

Thursday, November 5, 2015, began not much differently from any other day in the Hall household. Fourteen-month-old Brooklyn played happily while her grandparents watched over her and went about their daily routine.

Suddenly, there was a knock on the door.

It was the middle of the afternoon. Kathy was in the bedroom changing the baby's diaper. Jeff answered the door. The look on his face was anything but reassuring when he came to find Kathy.

She knew immediately something was wrong.

"DHS is at the door."

Kathy put Brooklyn into her crib, then went to the door.

A woman they had never seen before demanded, "Where's the baby?" She stood on the front porch flanked by two Fayetteville police officers. She informed them she was a social worker with DHS. Kathy refused to answer her until Jeff called the police department to confirm these people were indeed who they said they were.

The woman gave her name as Jamie Payton, but offered no explanation, other than to say she had been informed the baby's mother Hailey had left the state and abandoned her child. She insisted she must see Brooklyn immediately.

Kathy explained, "Ma'am, Hailey just went to her cousin's house for the weekend. She didn't abandon anybody." *There is no valid reason for these people to be here*, she thought to herself. *What kind of craziness is this?*

"I need to see Brooklyn now," Ms. Payton persisted.

Jeff went to get the baby. When he returned to the front door with Brooklyn, the social worker ordered him to hand the baby to her.

Kathy took Brooklyn from his arms. "I'm not just giving you my granddaughter!" She turned to the police. Her eyes pleaded with the officers. "I am not giving her to this woman."

"You have to." The officers explained they are there to keep the peace and make sure everything goes smoothly. However, they were adamant that Kathy and Jeff were required to give her the baby.

Neither the police nor the social worker had a court order or warrant.

The 4th Amendment of the United States Constitution states:

> The right of the people to be secure in their persons, houses, papers, and effects, against unreasonable searches and

seizures, shall not be violated, and no Warrants shall issue, but upon probable cause, supported by Oath or affirmation, and particularly describing the place to be searched, and the persons or things to be seized.

For the state to legally seize a child from their home without a warrant, the law says a child must be in "imminent danger." This exception allows law enforcement or social workers to intervene in cases where the child's life is in danger and there is no time to get a warrant from a judge and conduct a proper investigation.

That was not the case here, but Kathy and Jeff were not thinking about their Constitutional rights at the time. They were blindsided by the show of force standing on their doorstep. All they knew was that a stranger, backed up by men in uniform, was trying to take their grandchild.

Before this day, the Halls believed, like many Americans do, that Child Protective Services exists to protect children from parents who abuse and hurt their children, or are too drugged to take care of them. Like hundreds of thousands of others in the United States, they did not realize how mistaken they were until their own loved one was being ripped out of their lives.

Ms. Payton piped up, "Go get a diaper bag ready for her."

Kathy called Hailey on the phone so she could talk to the social worker. She'd been gone less than twenty-four hours, but Hailey told Ms. Payton she could fly back and be home within a couple of hours.

That wasn't good enough for Ms. Payton.

Hailey begged her not to take her baby. Her cries fell on deaf ears.

Ms. Payton said to give her a call when she got back into town; she would leave her number with Kathy. Meanwhile, she was taking the baby with her. Hailey would be able to take it up with the judge in court.

The sour-faced social worker again commanded Kathy to get a diaper bag together for the baby.

Devastated, Kathy set about trying to gather what Brooklyn would need. Tears quietly streamed down her face. She asked Ms. Payton what she could get for Brooklyn that would make it easier for her. "She's never been away from us," she explained.

The woman refused to answer.

"This doesn't even make sense to me. What else can I send with her to make this easier?"

Again, she gave no answer.

"She has never been away from any of us or her home," Kathy pleaded again. "Is there anything else that I can pack for my granddaughter to help make this easier for her?"

The woman refused to look at Kathy as she repeatedly asked for direction on what to send with Brooklyn.

Kathy was already upset, and the cross-eyed social worker's coldness was not helping. Finally in desperation, the words burst forth, "Would you please look at me with one of those two eyes you have going different ways and answer my question?"

The police spoke up then and informed them they had to get going.

"You can talk to the judge. Get the car seat," was the only response from the DHS worker, who apparently had a lazy eye condition.

Jeff got the car seat. He thought, *The police are here. We have to just let them take the baby, but surely she will be right back home.*

Reluctantly, Kathy handed Brooklyn over to Ms. Payton.

The social worker took the baby and the diaper bag from Kathy, and the entourage left. They had never stepped foot in the house, but they took the heart of the family with them when they left.

Kathy later said, "I was still under the impression that, when we got into court, everything would be explained, and Brooklyn would be brought right back home. I had no idea what was about to happen."

A Knock on the Door

3 - Big Misunderstanding, Right?

Hailey was on the next available flight to Arkansas. As soon as she arrived home, she immediately called the social worker.

"This whole thing is baloney," she told Ms. Payton. She had simply gone out of town to visit her cousin for a couple of days. She left her baby safely with her parents. There was no abandonment. She wanted to come to the DHS office to see Brooklyn right away.

"That is not going to happen," Ms. Payton informed her. Furthermore, if Hailey were to show up at the DHS office or try to meet with her before court, the social worker said she would have her taken into custody until she could speak to a judge.

Horrified and frightened, the seventeen-year-old called her mother. "Mom, they're going to put me in jail and I didn't even do anything!" Hailey was so scared she would not come home. Instead, she stayed in a hotel.

Kathy called the DHS office to find out when the hearing would be. Someone at DHS said they would notify them. Hailey called as well and got the same response.

Every day after Brooklyn was taken, Kathy and Hailey called DHS, asking when the hearing would be. Every day, they were told the same thing: "We'll let you know. We will notify you."

A couple of times, Kathy drove to the DHS office to inquire when the hearing was going to be. Each time, a woman at the front desk told her, "Hold on; let me check." She typed something into the computer as if to check, then responded, "There's nothing scheduled yet."

Most states have laws requiring the initial court hearing to be held within seventy-two hours of a child being seized. Arkansas law is no different, but Hailey and her parents did not know that. Unbeknown to them, a seventy-two-hour hearing did take place—on Monday, November 9, but they were never notified of the hearing or their right to be there.

By Monday, November 16, Brooklyn had been gone for a week and a half. There was still no word on any court hearing, and no one from the family had seen the baby. Kathy called Little Rock, the capitol of Arkansas, hoping to get someone higher up in DHS on the phone, to no avail.

Though they had already called DHS that morning and been told that nothing was scheduled yet, Kathy and Hailey decided once again to stop in at the DHS office. The woman who had normally been behind the desk every day they had gone in before was not there. A younger lady was there instead. It was around 2 p.m., and the staff was just getting back from lunch.

They asked the lady if the court hearing for Brooklyn was scheduled yet. She pulled something up on the computer and said, "Here it is. Yes, you have court today at four."

"What??" It was not the answer they expected. They got the details about where they needed to go, then rushed home to get cleaned up and dressed for court.

They expected everything to be straightened out once they appeared before a judge, and they would bring Brooklyn back home where she belonged. Courts, after all, are supposed to be about truth and justice—with presiding judges who are pillars of integrity in the community.

Kathy and Hailey would not be going to the regular courthouse where all the other judges heard their cases. Brooklyn's case was scheduled to be heard in the Washington County Juvenile Justice Center, about three miles away from the main courthouse. Judge Stacey Zimmerman, the sole juvenile court judge in the district since 1999, presided over the court.

They walked into the courthouse and through a metal detector. A police officer asked them what case they were there for. They told him. He directed them to wait for a moment.

The officer returned ten minutes later and handed them some papers. That is when they learned for the first time there had already been one court hearing on their case. They had missed the seventy-two-hour hearing on November 9. The documents showed they had been served notice and were aware of both hearings, but were not present in the first hearing. Clearly, this had not happened.

It is not uncommon for parents dealing with CPS to find false statements written in their court records saying they did not show up for a hearing (or a visit with their child), demonstrating to the court that the parent obviously did not care about the hearing.

One of the documents, Kathy later realized, showed notice of being served, complete with a signature and seal, but the part about where and when they were served was not filled out. They were not actually served until they showed up to court that day. They would never have been in the second hearing that day had it not been for the different receptionist who told them the truth.

The first thing Hailey saw on the top of one of the documents was the word "Adoption" typed in as the goal. Not reunification. Not placing Brooklyn with relatives. Just "Adoption." Hailey started crying.

Kathy tried to comfort her daughter. *Adoption isn't even an issue,* she thought. *Why is it even being discussed at this point?*

They sat outside the courtroom with the rest of the families waiting their turn to go in.

Big Misunderstanding, Right?

Like many family courts or juvenile courts across the nation, the courtroom was closed to all except those whose case was currently being heard. Unlike criminal courts, what happens in cases involving CPS usually happens behind closed doors. Those within the system often cite "confidentiality concerns," but advocates for victims of the system say the closed courts allow any misdeeds or corruption to be hidden behind a shroud of secrecy.

Meanwhile, Kathy believed the system worked and still had hope this was a simple misunderstanding which would be cleared up soon.

That was not going to be the case.

They were finally called into court at 7:00 p.m. In just five hours, Hailey would be eighteen years old. Judge Zimmerman appointed an attorney for Hailey, an attorney for Kathy, and assigned a case worker to the DHS case.

She told Hailey that if she would voluntarily enroll herself into foster care, she would get grants and state benefits which would help her, and she would receive additional legal help once she became an adult. If she agreed, the judge said the baby would immediately be placed into the same foster home with Hailey.

More than anything, Hailey wanted to be reunited with her baby. She agreed to submit to going into foster care as long as it meant she could be with Brooklyn.

Kathy's mind reeled with all this new information. First Brooklyn, and now Hailey, would not be home. She turned to the DHS workers and begged them to make sure Hailey continued in school. At the end of her pregnancy, Hailey had missed a month of classes when her doctor put her on bed rest. She was working very hard to catch up so she could graduate on time. The DHS workers insisted they would make sure Hailey did not miss school.

Immediately following court, Hailey was whisked away to a foster home assigned to her by Arkansas DHS. The foster home was located near the Missouri border, too far for her to continue attending her school. DHS made no attempt to enroll her into a new school.

They also never brought Brooklyn to the foster home.

DHS initially told Hailey they would bring the baby to her. Each time she asked, "When?" the workers said they were working on it.

After a week at the foster home without her baby and failed promises from DHS to bring Brooklyn to her, Hailey returned home to her family and school.

She told her mother about a disturbing conversation she had with her court-appointed attorney while at the foster home. Hailey had the attorney on speaker phone. She was, not surprisingly, upset about the whole situation, having her baby taken from her, being in a foster home, and DHS assuring her they would reunite them, then failing to do so. As she got more upset, and thus louder and louder over the phone, the attorney told her to calm down and listen to her.

Hailey had almost complete hearing loss in one ear—ninety-two percent—with eighty percent loss in the other ear. She had been this way since birth. Like many hearing-impaired people, Hailey's voice got louder and louder when she was upset or animated for any reason, even when she was happy or excited. To those who didn't know her, it could appear she was yelling, but she usually did not realize how loud she was getting.

Hailey missed hearing some of what the attorney was saying to her, but she heard this part clearly: "Well, if you would stop being a bitch—"

Hailey stopped her then and there. "You know what? You are not working for me." She hung up on her.

Kathy realized the attorney did not know about Hailey's hearing loss. She tried to call the attorney to explain. "I'm sorry, ma'am. I don't think you realize what's going on with my daughter."

"I have nothing to say to you. Hailey is my client, not you."

Kathy tried to explain to her that her daughter could not hear half of what she was saying because the conversation was over the phone. Hailey functioned in the hearing world largely by reading lips. The attorney did not seem to want to hear about it and came across as very rude to Kathy.

Hailey's case worker Haley Carson, however, was able to set up conversations with Hailey, the contents of which Kathy learned only later at a future hearing.

~ ~ ~

The next court hearing was held on December 3.

Hailey told Judge Zimmerman she did not like her attorney or the way her attorney talked to her.

The attorney responded that her client was disrespectful and would not listen to anything she had to say.

That was not the case. Hailey had a disability, and her mother repeatedly informed DHS and the court about her hearing loss. According to the Americans with Disabilities Act, both the court and DHS were required to make accommodations for her hearing loss. This never happened.

The judge ordered hair follicle drug tests for both Hailey and Brooklyn, even though there were no allegations of drug usage. This is another common practice in family and juvenile court cases. There was no history of drug use, either, but such history is not a prerequisite for drug testing to be ordered for people who become involved in the Child Protective system for any reason.

DHS told the court the foster parents they sent Hailey to could not accommodate a baby at their residence, nor could they find any foster home that would take both Hailey and Brooklyn together. This was not, however, what the foster parents told Hailey. They assured Hailey that Brooklyn was welcome at their home. They even volunteered to bring out their old baby crib and put it in Hailey's room for the baby.

Judge Zimmerman ordered the now eighteen-year-old Hailey back into foster care and ordered DHS to find a foster home for both Hailey and Brooklyn together.

Meanwhile, she ordered visitation be set up between Kathy Hall, Hailey King, and baby Brooklyn.

A staffing meeting to set up a parenting plan was scheduled to be held at the DHS building on December 18.

Immediately after court, DHS took Hailey to a foster home at Siloam Springs, on the Oklahoma border. Again, Brooklyn was not taken there.

Hailey's new foster care arrangement lasted all of two days because the DHS-approved foster parent touched her inappropriately. After notifying DHS about the incident, Hailey returned home to her family.

As bad as things were, they were about to get significantly worse.

4 - It's Not Supposed to Work This Way

There was still no evidence of abuse or neglect in the home, but the case proceeded as if Hailey were guilty of all allegations.

Hailey and Kathy met with DHS on December 18. DHS social workers gave her specific instructions she was required to follow. If she did not, the alternative plan was for Brooklyn's foster parents to adopt her.

In some states, this is called a "safety plan." In others, it is an "individualized service plan" or ISP. Some states refer to "participating in services." In Arkansas, it is known as a "parenting plan." No matter what they call it, it is essentially a list of requirements the parent must follow if they are to have any hope of getting their child or children back. The list can change throughout the process. As the parent jumps through hoops, social workers or judges can add more hoops, dangling the hope of restoration with their child like a carrot on a stick.

The list of requirements can range from something quite logical and expected, e.g. requiring a heroin addict to go through rehab and show clean drug tests, to the patently absurd.

The DHS list for Hailey included some of the latter. In addition to taking parenting classes, Hailey was required to demonstrate that she could financially support herself and her baby before Brooklyn could come home. This was to be done without any help from her family.

She had just turned eighteen a month before. She was still in her senior year of high school and had only worked part-time at fast food places. Yet, Child Protective Services forced her to move out on her own and support herself.

Not only is this something that the culture does not expect of teenagers who are still in school, it is quite the opposite of societal customs. Parents are generally expected to provide support for their children through the time they graduate from high school. Many families continue to help their grown children well into adulthood.

However, in CPS cases in many parts of the United States, young parents are often demanded to demonstrate financial independence, without any help from their parents, relatives, or the state, as a condition for their child returning home to them. It is an unrealistic, and largely unachievable, expectation.

In reflecting on this later, Kathy told a blog-show host, "I don't understand why that was even an issue. There's been a lot of families that have helped with the younger mothers until they're able to do it on their own. WE had no problem with it."[1]

DHS required Hailey and her mother to submit to drug testing, directing them to a specific lab. The agency generally contracts with certain labs in their area for all the drug testing.

Hailey's urine was screened on December 14 through Premier BioTech. It showed positive for THC, indicating marijuana usage. Hailey contested the screen. She had never used drugs, and she knew this could not be right.

DHS instructed Hailey to take Brooklyn with her to Omega Labs and have a hair drug test on herself and on her baby. The same lab tech took two hair samples each from Brooklyn and from Hailey, an hour apart on December 21.

Hailey's results came back two days later, showing negative for everything tested. Fourteen-month-old Brooklyn's results, on the other hand, took a week to come back. DHS told Hailey that the baby's test showed positive for THC and methamphetamines.

Hailey and Kathy could not understand what was happening. They did not realize at the time that there have been numerous labs around the U.S. and Canada that have been caught falsifying drug screening and test results, and people are in prison today for this. They only knew there was no way the results could be right.

Much later, one of their attorneys was accidentally given documents showing the test results DHS reported to the court, as well as the test results they did not report. When Kathy and her attorney realized what they had in their hands at that point, they could not believe the blatant fraud.

One of the documents shows the positive result, verified at 01:54 p.m. on 12/30/2015, from "Section B" of 1.5 inches of Brooklyn's hair. Another document, almost identical, shows a negative result, verified thirteen minutes earlier at 01:41 p.m., from "Section A" of 1.5 inches of Brooklyn's hair.

It is not possible for two sections of hair taken from the same person at the same time to show a different result. Either both are positive, or both are negative.

DHS also demanded Hailey's mother to submit to a urine drug screen. The screen showed positive for numerous things. However, a screen is not the same as a test. A screen does not differentiate between illicit drugs and prescription medications taken as properly prescribed. Kathy has lupus and epilepsy, and she was taking numerous medications prescribed by her doctor for her medical conditions. It is those medications which showed up on the screen, nothing more.

The truth did not seem to be the goal, however, and DHS reported all the positive results to the court.

~ ~ ~

The day before their next court appearance, Kathy was shocked to receive papers in the mail from DHS accusing her of abuse and neglect against Hailey and neglect of Brooklyn, signed by DHS investigator Jamie Payton. The papers said, "based on the preponderance of the evidence, the investigative agency determined the allegation to be true, and your name should be placed in the Child Maltreatment Central Registry."

There had been no hearing on these allegations, and no evidence presented by either side, yet the DHS investigator decreed in the papers that Kathy was guilty. This was the first Kathy or her attorney heard of the accusations.

When they got into the courtroom for the Probable Cause hearing, Hailey's case worker Haley Carson testified that baby Brooklyn had a small bruise on her head, indicating abuse. However, she was unable to provide any photos or evidence.

The case worker then testified that Hailey told her she had been abused by her mother.

Stunned, Kathy watched as her daughter took the stand. The DHS attorney asked her about the alleged abuse.

Hailey broke down into tears. "I'm not going to lie! My mom spanked me on the bottom one time, and it was one little swat on the butt when I ran in front of a car. Other than that, I've never been spanked my whole life. I've always been put in the corner."

She turned to the judge, distraught. "I know that this is not what they wanted me to say, but I'm not going to make these stories up about my mom."

She later told her mother her case worker and her attorney led her to believe that, if she made allegations of abuse against her parents, even if they were not true, she would get her baby back, with nothing being held against her. Hailey reluctantly went along with them in a moment of weakness, but ultimately she could not bring herself to allow her mother to be falsely accused.

Ms. Payton took the stand.

It's Not Supposed to Work This Way

Kathy's attorney asked her if DHS was trying to persuade Hailey to make up allegations against her mother.

She responded that she had forgotten her case file, but assured the court that DHS would never do something like that.

The attorney asked her if she would like to retrieve the case file before going any further. She said she did not need it.

"Did Hailey make any claims of abuse against her mother?"

"No."

"Did you file any charges against Kathy Hall?"

"No."

"Are you certain of that, Ms. Payton? Do you want to get your case file to make sure before you answer that question?"

The DHS investigator was given at least four opportunities to leave and retrieve the case file on Hailey King, but she insisted it was not necessary. She continued to deny that any allegations were filed against Hailey's mother.

She squirmed a bit in her seat when Kathy's attorney handed her a set of papers. Kathy suspected Ms. Payton did not believe the mail would have delivered them already and was thus surprised to see the documents. "Would you read this, and state for the court whose signature is written on the bottom?"

It was indeed her signature, but she said she did not remember signing it.

The attorney then produced paperwork they had received from DHS which contained the false allegations used to remove Brooklyn from the home. Ms. Payton had written that the Halls had no food in the house and the utilities had been cut off.

The Halls had letters from the utility companies showing they had never been disconnected. The attorney provided these to the court.

Ms. Payton had never been inside their home in order to make any determination of whether there was food in the house or not. In fact, Brooklyn was taken at the beginning of the month, right after Jeff received his monthly military pension. Bank statements showing how much they had just spent at the grocery store for lots of food were entered into evidence.

By the time it was over, it was clear the DHS investigator had lied in order to seize Brooklyn, and continued to lie about the case repeatedly, even on the stand. The subsequent allegations against Kathy appeared to be a not-so-transparent attempt to disqualify the Halls for kinship placement.

Despite all of this, Brooklyn was not returned home to her mother, nor to her grandparents. The foster parents had been present for the hearing and would again be taking the baby home with them.

Hailey had an aunt in Texas who was a state-approved foster parent. She and several other relatives offered to take care of Brooklyn, but the court never considered placing Brooklyn with any family members.

This is a story repeated all over America—children removed by CPS are routinely placed with, and adopted out to, strangers, despite multiple family members offering to care for their loved one. Social workers routinely tell courts there were no suitable relative placements found, despite some of them having already been approved or licensed by the state as foster, or even adoptive, parents for other people's children within the CPS system. Part of the reason for this is the Adoption and Safe Families Act of 1997, which provides billions of dollars of federal funds to states out of Social Security—Title IV-E—for adopting children out to non-family members. This particular stream of funding is not available when children are returned home to their families or adopted by relatives.

Judge Zimmerman reiterated to Hailey that the court did not want her to live at home because she needed to prove to DHS and to her that she was capable of living on her own and supporting herself. Meanwhile, she ordered Hailey to attend drug rehab in Bentonville, Arkansas. She assured Hailey that Brooklyn would eventually be reunited with her there.

Kathy later learned Brooklyn's foster father served on the board of the facility as their assistant accountant, and later their accountant.

Caseworker Haley Carson testified there was a room open and available at the facility for both Hailey and the baby. That did not prove to be the case.

The judge dismissed Kathy's attorney. She ordered the case be termed a "reunification" case; therefore, Kathy Hall would no longer be considered a party to the case. (In later hearings, however, DHS clearly expected Kathy to be present. She believes this was an excuse to get rid of her attorney because she showed the courage and integrity to fight for her client.)

Judge Zimmerman was also reportedly not very happy with Ms. Payton. She asked her to stay behind after the hearing.

Ms. Payton was no longer employed by the Department of Human Services by the next day, but perhaps that is just a coincidence.

To date, no charges of perjury have been filed against her or anyone else involved in the case for lying under oath.

Child Protective Services DATA

Less than 16% of children are taken from their families for reasons of any kind of abuse—physical or sexual. This figure has been consistent for several years, according to data from the annual AFCARS Report from the U.S. Department of Health and Human Services, Administration for Children and Families, Administration on Children, Youth and Families, Children's Bureau.

www.acf.hhs.gov/sites/default/files/documents/cb/afcars-report-29.pdf

Only about 17% of all allegations against parents are substantiated (and substantiation can occur without any actual evidence.) This figure has remained within a few tenths of a percentage point for the past several years. This data is available in the annual Child Maltreatment Report from the Children's Bureau, Administration on Children, Youth and Families, Administration for Children and Families, U.S. Department of Health and Human Services.

www.acf.hhs.gov/sites/default/files/documents/cb/afcars-report-29.pdf

5 - Downward Spiral

There was not an immediate opening at the rehab facility as they had been told by the social worker.

"Mom, no matter what I do, they're never going to give Brooklyn back." Though Hailey tried to do everything the court demanded of her, she was quickly losing hope any of it made a difference.

Hailey and Kathy were able to visit with Brooklyn—for two hours a week. Every Tuesday a DHS worker supervised their visits at Chick-Fil-A. These visits were precious, but not nearly long enough. Hailey and Kathy often fought to hide their tears when they saw what little Brooklyn was going through.

Sometimes the baby showed up with bruises on her face, usually in the same place. DHS explained that they were from accidental falls. The foster father was, they were told, legally blind, and "accidents happen." Brooklyn kept a bleeding diaper rash. Before she was taken, she had never had a diaper rash.

Though it was winter, there were times she showed up at visits with no shoes on her feet. Hailey and Kathy frequently brought clean clothes, shoes, and hair bows for Brooklyn to their visits.

Hailey and Kathy consistently reported the baby's injuries, but those reports never seemed to make it into the DHS records.

There was one visit Hailey did not attend. She was sick with a cough and a fever, and she did not want to risk making her child sick. Kathy held Brooklyn in her arms as she explained this to the social worker. It was cold outside the restaurant, but it did not compare to the coldness in Haley Carson's voice. "I don't care where she is or what she is doing; I'm going to make sure that neither you or anybody in your family ever gets that baby back."

Hailey grew increasingly hopeless and desperate. She could not live at home if she had any hope of meeting DHS demands and getting Brooklyn back.

"Mom, what am I going to do? Now I am going to have to drop out of school so I can make enough money to get my baby back. There's nothing I can do that's going to make enough money to pay rent, pay for utilities, and pay for childcare. There's nothing I can do, short of going to college, and by then they won't give her back to me!"

Kathy was devastated, and she had no idea how to help her daughter. DHS and Judge Zimmerman had tied her hands.

Hailey descended into a downward spiral. Within a month, Kathy watched her youngest child, who she described as one "who has always done just about everything right," drop out of school and start stripping at a club to try to make enough money to support herself. It was the only job she could find that paid enough for her to live on her own. Soon after, a guy she met at the strip club introduced her to drugs. The people in that world nick-named her "London" because of the way she talked.

She stopped calling home or coming to the house. Before DHS came into her life, she had never been on drugs, and she had never been away from home for longer than a three-day weekend during her entire life.

Every passing day with her baby in DHS custody, Hailey sank deeper and deeper into despair.

~ ~ ~

The next time they went to court, Kathy pleaded with the judge to get her daughter into rehab and get her counseling. She also asked for a CASA (Court Appointed Special Advocate) worker to be assigned to her daughter.

When Kathy's family had lived in Colorado before moving to Arkansas, she had taken in the children of a family member when the family was going through a tough season. She had seen foster care workers and CASA workers who were helpful, not harmful, to the children they were involved with. She never dreamed there was a darker side to the system until DHS took Brooklyn. Kathy still held out hope that, perhaps, a volunteer CASA worker could help Hailey and get her out of the destructive spiral she was in.

Judge Zimmerman ordered DHS to set up counseling for Hailey.

They were still waiting for a spot to open up for Hailey at the rehab facility, they said, but it had not happened yet.

Meanwhile, the Hall family downsized from their big, beautiful home to a less expensive duplex in a cul-de-sac not far from their former neighborhood, so they could afford to hire an attorney to help get their family back together after Judge Zimmerman dismissed their former attorney.

~ ~ ~

The last time Hailey was in court was in May of 2016. Judge Zimmerman took one look at Hailey and said she looked like a shell of her former self.

It was true. The system had broken her.

Tearfully, Kathy again begged the judge to get Hailey into a drug rehab program and help her before something happened to her. Her daughter was falling apart before her eyes, and she was powerless to stop it.

The judge appointed a CASA worker for Hailey and ordered her to return back home to her parents and work on getting her GED until DHS could get her into rehab.

Kathy was floored. She later described[1] what she thought in that moment. "Now that they've destroyed her life, and her life has gone downhill, now they're telling her they want her to go back home, and for us to be helping her? I couldn't believe what I was hearing after they've done all of this!"

When they got home, Hailey burst into tears. "Why couldn't they have ordered me in the beginning to stay at home and go to school? I had a roof over my head, and a happy family with all the support I ever needed to be a good mother and have a good future with my baby!"

Why, indeed? Kathy struggled to find a way to answer her, but any rational explanation eluded her.

Hailey was finally able to come back home, but so much damage had already been done. Hailey had gone places and done things she never dreamed of before DHS came into her life. She had become mixed up with people who were not good for her at all.

The new CASA worker met with Hailey at Kathy's house one time. She said she was brand new to CASA and bragged she been trained by none other than Haley Carson. The social worker had quit her job with DHS after the last court hearing and went to work for the CASA program.

Kathy's heart sank. It was clear her daughter would find no help with CASA.

Before all of this happened, Kathy truly believed in the system. Not anymore. Disillusioned and heartbroken, she felt she had been very naive in trusting that CPS was about protecting children or helping families. She gave up on the idea of the courts trying to help them.

Hailey wanted to get better. Once she was home, she started reading her Bible again. She documented in her Bible that she accepted Jesus as her Savior on July 22, 2016. She was baptized on July 31. It was a long road back, but she was trying to turn her life around.

One horrible day that summer, Jeff and one of Hailey's brothers got phone calls to pick up Hailey. After they brought her home, Kathy asked where she was. They couldn't find her. Kathy found her curled up in a ball, crying, hiding in the closet beneath the stairs. There was blood on her shorts and thighs. It was apparent she had been raped, but she was too traumatized to talk about it.

Kathy immediately called the DHS caseworker and got her voicemail. She left a message, but she never got a response. She called the CASA worker, who told her there was nothing they could do. She suggested calling the police, but Hailey would not talk.

DHS was court-ordered months before to get her into counseling, but that had not happened. Kathy asked again for a counselor, but DHS said it was not their responsibility. Neither DHS nor CASA would help get a referral for Hailey.

Kathy and Jeff knew it was up to them to get help for Hailey, especially after this latest trauma. They talked with Hailey, who agreed she needed to check into a mental health hospital. She was ready to start facing her demons.

Hailey had become very fearful. In the hospital, she told the staff she knew something was going to kill her. One of her assignments was to write strategies for overcoming her fear. On one worksheet she wrote affirmations that she must tell herself daily. She concluded with the statement, "As long as I follow this, I have nothing to be afraid."

For another worksheet, she drew pictures of how others see her versus how she sees herself. On one of these, she saw herself with wings.

On another, she contrasted others seeing her as strong, capable, and happy, while she saw herself looking like death, with bloody wounds on her face and head.

Her therapists at the hospital said she had schizophrenic ideologies from drugs, but her drug tests showed she was clean. They told Hailey her fear was all in her head.

As it turned out, the fear was not in her head at all. A group of thugs showed up at the Hall's house in late August—not long after Hailey got home from the hospital. When Kathy answered the door, they demanded to see Hailey. They made their intentions to harm her clear.

They were standing in the doorway, so Kathy couldn't shut the door. She is petite—only 4'10". There was one of her and several of them, and they refused to leave. They threatened to kill Hailey and said they were going to shoot up the house.

Kathy could not get to her phone because it was upstairs. However, her handgun was accessible, and she got it out. She did not mince words with them. With her voice low and steady, she said, "I'm not going to tell you again to get the hell off of my property."

When the police arrived, they asked what happened. After one of the officers went to his car and made a phone call, he came back and charged her with a felony for brandishing a gun.

Her lawyer agreed it was clearly a case of self-defense. No shots had been fired, and she could easily have beaten the case if she took it to court. He told Kathy her name was flagged in the computer because of the DHS case. Police in the area, he said, had been known to be instructed by DHS to make charges against people who are involved with the agency, whether or not they deserve the charges. It made it easier for the court to keep the children in DHS custody if the parent or relative had a pending felony against them.

Kathy found herself between a rock and a hard place. She was advised she could not have a pending felony and have any chance to get Brooklyn placed with her. She ultimately agreed to plead guilty to a lesser charge of a misdemeanor instead of fighting the charge, in the hope of bringing the baby home. She did it for Brooklyn.

Kathy later said, "I didn't know then that it wouldn't matter because they weren't going to give me custody no matter what. If I would've known that, I would've fought the charges, but I didn't."

Things finally started to look like they were turning around for Hailey. She was home, and she was loved. She was dealing with things. She left behind her "London" persona and finally starting to feel like Hailey King again.

She wrote a letter to Brooklyn, dated October 29, 2016.

…Brooklyn is gone. Damit, and I can't live with the pain of her not here anymore. I cry every night wishing I could hold her one more time. I can't breath without my heart. I love her more than anything in this entire world. She is who makes me Hailey again. She is my daughter. And i'm dying. Slowly.

Brooklyn, please forgive me when you grow up. Please remember when you laid on my chest naked and warm to calm your heart. Please remember me having to have you to where our faces were touching, sleeping so I knew you were okay….Brooklyn, I can't forget you. I can't live without you. I love you so much babygirl.

You are my sunshine, my lovely sunshine. You make me happy when the clouds are grey. Oh what I do know is that your my sunshine. So please lord bring my sunshine <u>back</u> today.

Babygirl, I love you. So very much.

I Love you.

xoxo Mommy

Downward Spiral

6 - Sirens, and More Sirens

Tinkerbell to Peter Pan
"You know that place between sleep and awake, that place where you can still remember dreaming? That's where I will always love you. That's where I will be waiting." – Hailey's favorite quote

Kathy Hall reflects on the loss of a child:

> Every single thing they've ever touched, we try to hold onto. It's like, why don't we stop before you lose them and treasure the stupid little things more, that we just take for granted…stuff that I normally would have tossed in the trash—and now, it means everything.
>
> I know it's weird. I've thought about that a lot. And I've gone back a million times too, saying, What if I would have done this different that day? or What if I would have done that? But you know, that day was like any normal day. She said she was going to go with her friends. She'd be back in time for dinner.

And it was, "Get out of my closet; leave my clothes alone." Like you do with most teenagers. And for a long time I kept thinking, and after she died that night, I kept saying, why didn't I just let her take one of my sweatshirts? Why was I figh—— [voice trails off] She was LEAVING. That's why—so much goes through your mind.

~~~

It was a week after Hailey wrote the letter to her daughter, November 6, 2016—a year and a day since DHS took Brooklyn from her home. Hailey went out with friends on Sunday afternoon and told her mom she would be home in time for dinner.

Close to dinnertime, Kathy and Jeff heard sirens coming from down the street.

Kathy had a sinking feeling those sirens were for Hailey and there was something wrong. *I just knew. I've known every time when there's something wrong with my kids.*

Jeff knew his wife well enough to know what she was thinking. "I am not going down there."

About that time, the doorbell rang. Hailey's friend Lauren[1] stood on the doorstep asking for Hailey.

Kathy said, "She's not here."

More sirens blared in the distance. It sounded like several vehicles.

Kathy asked, "What in the heck is going on?"

"Oh my God. I was right behind it. Some guy was crossing the street. He got hit, and his body—" Lauren shuddered. "I've never seen a body twisted like a pretzel like that in my life."

Kathy felt like she was going to throw up. "Jeff—"

He knew what she was going to say, and he tried to reassure her. "She said it was a boy."

"I didn't get close enough, but, yeah, it was a boy. You could see like some black shoes laying out in the street. It was so weird, and, oh my God, I think they're dead."

"Are you sure it wasn't Hailey?

"No, it wasn't Hailey." Lauren looked around Kathy, "Where is she?"

"I don't know," Kathy responded. "She should have already been here. She was supposed to be home for dinner."

Kathy tried calling Hailey, but she didn't answer her phone.

They heard more sirens. Kathy opened the door, and it sounded like the sirens were going away.

Jeff said, "They are already leaving."

"I have such a bad feeling, Jeff. Please go up there and check and see if that's her."

She tried to bring herself to walk over to see what was going on, but she could not do it. She later wondered if it was God trying to stop her. She backed away from the door.

Jeff did not believe the sirens had anything to do with Hailey, and he did not see any need to check it out.

Kathy tried again to go, but she could not get anywhere near the front door without shaking and feeling like she was going to throw up and pass out at the same time.

"Jeff, PLEASE," she implored. "Go see what is happening."

When he opened the door to go, they heard a whole new set of sirens coming. They had just heard sirens leaving, but these sounded like they were coming back. Kathy had never before had a panic attack, but she felt like she was having one. Her heart raced.

Sirens, and More Sirens

After Jeff left, she turned back to Lauren. "Are you sure it was a boy you saw?"

"Yes. I just talked to her and she was on her way back here. We were going to go see a movie. That's why I'm here. I was picking her up."

Kathy got even more uneasy then. Hailey was still not home. Her mother's intuition told her something was very, very wrong.

It was not long before Jeff came back home. "They wouldn't let me get anywhere near, but they said some boy got hit out there. It's not Hailey. She wouldn't be walking down the street. You know your daughter."

"Ok, ok, ok, ok." Kathy tried to breathe easier, but she kept hearing the sirens. Every siren she heard made her panic more. Another siren came toward them again, and then went away.

Lauren waited about forty-five minutes because she was still upset and shaken by the body lying in the street. She told them she was the third car to pull up on the scene. "Somebody went over and put a blanket or something over him, and I had to wait awhile till I could back up because—" She said she just got so freaked out, she couldn't go over there to try to help. "There were already people around him." She drove past the accident and continued the half mile to her friend's house.

Hailey never came home, and she never answered her phone.

About 9:30 that evening the phone rang. Someone from the rehab facility called and said they finally had an open bed. They wanted Hailey there the next morning. Kathy texted her daughter, "[The rehab facility] called, and you need to get home because we've got to get you packed. We've got to leave here first thing in the morning to get you up there. They've finally got a bed."

There was no response.

Kathy finally climbed upstairs to bed to try to shut out her fears, but she couldn't sleep.

She was still lying awake in bed when Jeff came in at 12:15 a.m. "Babe, Melanie's[2] here looking for Hailey. I think you need to talk to her."

Melanie was one of Hailey's friends Kathy did not trust. *Why in the world did he just let that girl in our house?* She sat up in bed and turned on the light as Melanie walked into the room. It was obvious she had been crying.

"Please tell me Hailey is here. Please, please tell me she's here."

Now Kathy was really scared. "No, she's not. What is wrong?"

"I'm just looking for her."

Just then Jeff appeared back in the doorway. "Babe, I think Hailey got her ass in trouble. There's a couple of detectives at the door for you. They want to talk to you."

Kathy looked at him, then looked again at Melanie. Tears started to roll down Melanie's face. Kathy turned back to Jeff, and said quietly, "She didn't get in trouble. She's dead. I told you that was her earlier."

Jeff shook it off. "Give me a break."

Kathy made her way down the stairs and opened the door to two plainclothes officers and two officers in uniform. The first words out of her mouth were, "Is she dead or alive?"

"Ma'am, we're not even sure it's her that we have."

Kathy felt like she could not breathe. She stepped outside with them and shut the door behind her. Jeff stayed inside the house, convinced Hailey had gotten into some kind of trouble, never dreaming Kathy's forebodings were correct.

The officers peppered her with questions. Do you have a daughter? How old is she? What's her birth date? Does she have any tattoos or marks on her body?

She tried to remember the tattoos Hailey had, most of which she had just started the process of removing. "She's got Tom and Jerry." She struggled to think of the various cartoons her daughter had tattooed on her. *I can't think!*

As she named them, she could see she was not saying anything they recognized. She started to get a little bit hopeful that maybe this wasn't Hailey.

"Does she have any names or numbers or anything like that on a tattoo?"

Sirens, and More Sirens

Think, think, think, Kathy. Then it hit her. "She has Brooklyn right here," and she pointed just below her collarbone.

The police officer put his head down and said, "You need to come with me."

Kathy slid down the wall. "Is she dead or alive?"

"Ma'am, I can't tell you anything except for the doctors want to talk to you."

Kathy tried desperately to think logically. Her husband was in the Army. *If they come to the door, it's usually because they're dead. Then again, they don't take you to the hospital if they're dead.*

Then it hit her. She just knew. She opened the door and called out, "Jeff, grab my shoes. Grab my cell phone. Grab your shoes. We've gotta go."

"It's late," he complained. "I'm not going anywhere."

Kathy said, "Hailey is in the hospital. She is going to die. She's brain dead." She did not know how she knew. She just knew.

Jeff was puzzled. "What?"

One of the officers stepped in. "You need to come with your wife."

Jeff realized this was serious. He quickly gathered their shoes and cell phones. He and Kathy followed the officers and climbed into the back of a police car. All during the ride to the hospital, Kathy told herself, *Ok, she's in the hospital, and she hasn't died.* She tried to convince herself not to think the worst as they rode up the elevator to the ICU. *It can't be; she's still alive.*

She questioned the officer escorting them through the hospital. "I heard a lot of sirens earlier and somebody was hit crossing the street or something. Was that it?"

"I don't know all the details. It happened a while ago. There was another victim. He's at the hospital as well."

"What took you so long to get to me? I was a block away."

"I don't know. I just came on duty and I was asked to come and bring the family in. That's all I know."

"Oh my God." She realized right then she was right about something she desperately wanted to be wrong about. "She couldn't tell you who she was."

They stood outside of ICU with several detectives for what seemed like an eternity. It was probably only ten or fifteen minutes. The nurses knew they were there.

Kathy tried to open the door to the ICU, but it was locked. "What is going on? Open the door. Let me in to see my child."

An officer attempted to calm her down, "Ma'am, the doctors need to talk to you."

"I don't care about the doctors. Somebody needs to come out here and open this door."

"They will be right out."

She noticed some people laying down in the waiting area with blankets over them. She could tell they were awake, but they did not sit up or acknowledge the other people who were there. *Are they connected to the other victim?*

One of the officers asked her if she knew someone named David Gutierrez or knew any of Hailey's friends who drove a scooter. She did not. He asked about a young Hispanic man of medium build, but his description did not sound familiar to Kathy.

A few more minutes ticked by. Kathy headed to the door of the ICU. "I'm not waiting another minute." She glared at one of the officers. "You go open that damn door or I'm going to kick it in. Period. Arrest me if you want, but I'm kicking in that f*ing door."

At that moment, the doors opened. Doctors and nurses poured through the ICU doors and another back door Kathy had not noticed before. What seemed like at least twenty people swarmed around Kathy and Jeff, forming a circle around them. Kathy's heart raced and she thought she was going to pass out.

She tried to listen as words swirled around her: internal bleeding, brain injury, brain stem hemorrhage, she'll never wake up, non-survivable. The words made no sense. All she could think was, *Get the hell away from me and take me to my kid!*

One voice broke through the noise. "What do you want us to do? She has already coded three times. We've given her two blood transfusions. We cannot keep her heart beating even on the life support without the blood being able to flow, and we can't sustain the loss of blood that's going on."

Kathy tried to focus, to absorb the words coming at her. She asked, "Are there any brain waves?"

"No. None."

They needed to know what Kathy, as next of kin, wanted them to do. "It's not a matter of if her heart stops again; it's a matter of when."

"I'm not going to give you that answer. Take me to my child," Kathy insisted. "I'll make up my mind when the time comes. But I want to see her."

7 - Hailey

She expected to walk into the room and find her daughter battered and mangled with machines everywhere. She and Jeff found Hailey lying in the bed with a neck brace and a breathing tube in her mouth. There were two IV bags and a heart monitor attached to her, beeping. She could not see the gash that went all the way through the top of her daughter's head because that part of her head was angled away from her.

A nurse directed her not to touch her daughter except for her hand, due to the bleeding and open wounds.

Hailey's eyes were wide open.

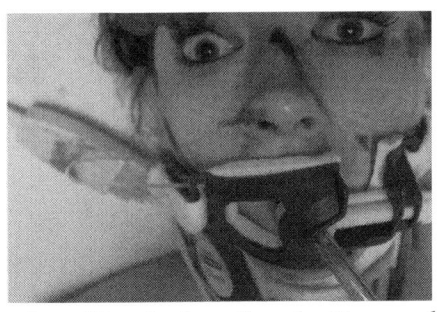

The nurse spoke to her. "You look really pale. You need to sit, right here. Just touch her hand and talk to her and be with her."

Kathy took her baby girl's hand. Her knuckles were badly skinned. She told Hailey how much she loved her, how much she means to her.

The whole time Kathy talked to her, Hailey never blinked. Kathy understood in that moment what it means to say, "the lights were on, but nobody was home."

"Is she sedated?"

"No, ma'am. We haven't sedated her." She told Kathy her heart had already stopped three times, and they didn't think they were going to be able to resuscitate the last time it stopped.

"Has there been anything from her, any movement, anything? A moan?"

"No, ma'am." She explained she had been Hailey's nurse in the emergency room also. She had accompanied her to the CAT scan and other tests. She had not seen any response from Hailey.

The doctors said that even if there were a miracle and somehow Hailey's heart didn't stop again, she would be in this state the rest of her life. She would never be able to breathe on her own because it was a brain stem hemorrhage. She would have to be on a ventilator the rest of her life.

Kathy sat with Hailey for about a half hour before she tried to make any calls. She needed to call Hailey's father and her other children. They told her she could not use her cell phone in the ICU room, but Kathy refused to leave Hailey's side. They said she could use the phone at the nurse's station. She could still see her from there.

Jeff went outside to smoke a cigarette, and Kathy made her calls. She walked back into the room and sat by Hailey's side again, broken.

"Hailey, I don't know what to do. I can't tell them to not try to save you. I can't bring myself to do it, but I can't leave you like this the rest of your life."

Kathy's mind raced as she tried to figure out what to do. *If I were to make them save her, and the bleeding could stop, the only reason she would still be alive is because of this machine breathing for her. Would this only be for me? That's no kind of life for her. On the other hand,* she thought, *how can I reason out the fact that I didn't try to save my child either?*

She talked to Hailey and told her, "You've got to help me here. I don't know what to do. If you're going to fight, and you think you can survive, then you fight. But if you can't, go ahead and let go. Because I can't make this call. I can't do it."

By this time Kathy was crying hysterically.

She got up and went to the nurse's station once again to try to reach Hailey's father. As she started to leave him a message, all of a sudden a calm came over her. She hung up the phone without leaving a message.

She matter-of-factly told the nurse at the desk, "She's going."

She got half way between the nurse's station and the room when she heard an insistent "beep, beep, beep, beep."

She walked into Hailey's room and said, "Get my husband." Jeff was just coming off the elevator. They rushed him into the room with Kathy. People came running into the room with the crash cart there. The doctors asked, "What do you want us to do?"

Kathy looked down at her child and held her hand. She could feel her all over in that room, but she already knew Hailey wasn't in that body.

She asked, "Is there even a one percent chance?"

The doctor met her eyes and shook his head. "I'm sorry."

Kathy looked at Hailey again and told her she loved her, then looked up at the doctor, "Let her go in peace."

As Hailey's heart was stopping, Kathy made a vow to her daughter. "I promise you, I will get justice for you for who did this to you, and I will fight to bring Brooklyn home, to be raised every day to know who her mommy was and how much she loved her. I will fight till my last breath. I will never stop."

She sat with her youngest daughter until her heart stopped at 1:45 a.m. She ran out of the room and kept running, blinded by her tears.

Hailey

~ ~ ~

At some point, she fell on the ground on the sidewalk in front of the hospital. She remembers screaming and cursing at God. "If You are this almighty, powerful God, how could You let this happen?" She was very angry that He allowed all this to happen with Hailey and with Brooklyn, and for Hailey to die, knowing that Brooklyn hadn't made it home. She poured out her anger and grief to the God who is big enough to handle our pain.

She then tried to bargain with God, telling Him to take her instead because Hailey had her whole life still ahead of her.

After about twenty minutes, Hailey's friend Angela[1] came outside searching for Kathy. "You've got to get up off this ground and stop screaming. Your daughter needs you. You need to go up there and say your goodbyes to her."

That is exactly what she needed to do. Kathy knew she was right. Angela was a real source of strength to her that night. "Come on. You can cry later, but come on. Right now you've got to go. She needs you right now."

Kathy got up and wiped away the tears. By the time she got back to Hailey's room, hospital staff had just finished up disconnecting everything. They didn't take the neck brace and the thing off her mouth yet, but they closed her eyes.

Kathy thought, *NOW you closed her eyes? You couldn't close her f*ing eyelids before I came in and saw that?* To this day she still dreams about her wide-open, vacant eyes in the hospital.

Jeff and Kathy talked to her for a long time, telling her how much they loved her.

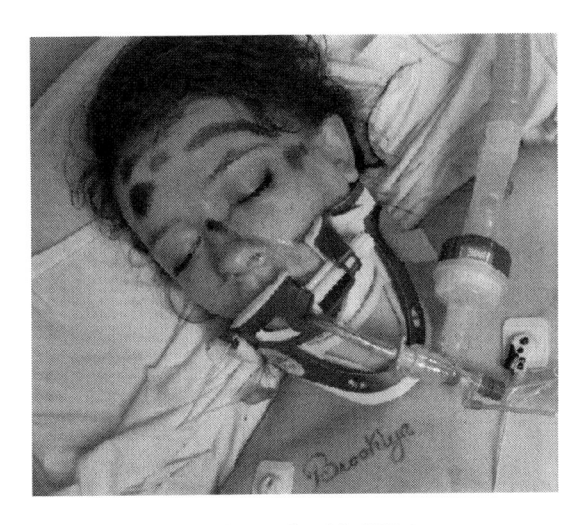

Finally, Jeff looked over at Kathy and said, "We've got to get your stuff and get you home. You don't look good."

"Leave me alone. Don't talk to me." By this point she felt like she was angry with everybody. She did not want anybody to touch her, look at her, or talk to her. She just wanted to be left alone.

They walked back out by the waiting room and saw friends crying. She noticed the people still lying there that she noticed earlier, but no one spoke to them.

Nurses came out and said, "We need you to sign this form," and "We need you to call a funeral home."

That's weird. I thought the coroner would come get her and whatever, and she'd have an autopsy.

Then somebody said something else to her and she had to sign this and sign that. "Who am I supposed to call?"

Someone said to make sure she calls for someone to pick Hailey's body up. Kathy felt like her brain was going in twenty different directions. *Who am I supposed to call? I don't know a funeral home around here.*

The room started spinning; she felt lightheaded.

The next thing she knew, she woke up in the emergency room with wires and machines attached to her, surrounded by extremely attentive nurses. She sat up and ripped the wires off of her. It seemed to Kathy the nurses were looking at her quite pitifully.

"Ma'am, your blood pressure is so high. You need to stay here."

She felt like the walls were closing in on her. "I'm sure it is. My child just died. I've got to get out of this room and out of this hospital."

She raced outside to get some air.

One of the detectives told her later those were the same nurses who tried to save Hailey in the ER.

It was close to 3 a.m. before they got home, but Kathy was too upset to sleep well.

At 5:30 a.m., someone pounded on her door. *Who could this possibly be this early in the morning?*

8 - David

Kathy opened her door to find news reporters and cameras. They wanted statements from the family of the hit-and-run victim. Police were searching for a man who was on the run after killing one person and leaving another in critical condition.

As details emerged over the next days, weeks, and months about the events that took place that night, it became clear this was much more than a horrible accident. A violent crime had taken place. Not only did it take Hailey's life, it also resulted in a young man losing both his legs.

Kathy's instincts were right. The people she saw in the waiting room were connected to what happened to Hailey. They were the friends and family of another victim who was with Hailey when she was hit.

According to police reports, Hailey was the passenger on a motor scooter driven by twenty-year-old Osmin David Gutierrez. They were heading south on North Crossover Road. Another couple of blocks and they would have reached Hailey's house. They were in the left-hand lane on a straightaway in a thirty-five mph speed zone. Traffic was light, and road conditions were clear.

Suddenly the scooter was slammed from behind by a red Chevrolet Silverado truck at 6:59 p.m. Investigators said Hailey was thrown up onto the hood of the extended-cab pickup truck and carried for approximately two-hundred thirty-five feet. Without any sign of slowing down, the truck swerved into the right-hand lane, throwing Hailey off. She landed onto the ground in front of the Fayetteville Athletic Club. David and the scooter were trapped between the engine of the truck and the road, but the truck kept going.

An employee at the athletic club was taking the trash out and saw sparks flying as the truck sped by. When he realized an accident had occurred, he ran to the victim he saw lying in the road. Hailey lay face down with her arm twisted at an angle that was all wrong. She was breathing, but not conscious. The employee waved his hands to stop traffic until help arrived.

A video camera at the athletic club captured the impact. The truck was going at least seventy-one mph when it hit them. There was no evidence the driver of the truck ever hit the brakes or slowed down. Sparks flew for a considerable distance as the scooter gouged the asphalt.

The truck paused briefly as it rounded the corner onto East Zion Road, still dragging David and the scooter under it. They passed a Mexican restaurant and Piney Ridge Treatment Center for juveniles before David was finally dislodged from under the truck as it turned left into the entrance of Valley Lake Apartments. He had been dragged over twenty-two hundred feet, almost half a mile.

His legs were mangled and he lay in a pool of his own blood, but he was still awake and conscious, screaming for help.

The driver pulled into a parking spot behind the office of the apartment complex, with the scooter still under the truck.

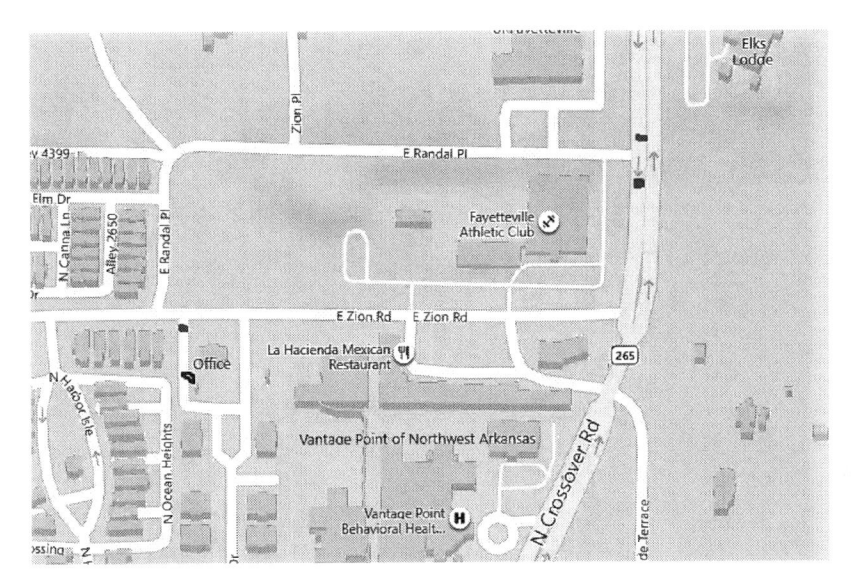

He then backed out and pulled into another parking spot. He had to have heard David's cries for help when he got out of his truck, but he ignored them. He hid an ice chest of beer in the bushes by the office, then vanished into the night. He never tried to call for help for his victims.

Multiple 911 calls came in that night about the crash. The first caller saw Hailey in the road and pulled over to help. He did not see what happened, but said he "literally was leaving a Bible study and saw the person laying on the road and stopped. I'm blocking traffic." He told the 911 dispatcher it looked like a young man, maybe twenty years old. The person was breathing but not awake. "He's moaning, but I don't know what's broken. I don't want to move him. His shoes are off." He thought Hailey was a boy who had been hit by a bike.

The video surveillance camera showed that Hailey's friend Lauren's car passed the scene of the crash on her way to the Hall's house less than two minutes after she was hit. Emergency vehicles arrived on the scene moments later.

One of the first people on the scene was a doctor who had been driving by, but he did not see the accident. He told Kathy the medics intubated her in the ambulance, but they did not need sedation to do so because she was unconscious. "I don't think she even knew what hit her."

Another man phoned 911 about David. He saw an ambulance down the block by Hailey, then rounded the corner and saw David lying in the entrance of the apartments. He described a kid who looked "like his legs are smashed off." David was "screaming for help before anyone ran up to him. His legs are all ran over, looks like they're detached from him."

The 911 dispatcher was confused and asked questions to clarify where the accident was. At that point dispatchers did not realize there were two accident scenes, not just one.

A third caller arrived on the scene and saw David lying in a huge pool of blood. She called 911 and said, "He's trying to get up, and there's no way he can." The dispatcher said they were redirecting emergency vehicles "to the right area." Just then another lady told the caller on the phone she had to turn around because there was another accident just down the road. "Oh," the caller said, "apparently someone else got hit, too.

Police officers on the way to Hailey were notified that first responders had reached her. Her condition was critical, and there was a second victim. The officers were rerouted to David. They reported that David's legs were flat when they arrived at 7:07 p.m. His legs had detached, but David didn't yet realize he couldn't use his legs.

He tried to push himself up on his elbows, and said he needed help with his legs. He said, "They're after me. They're after me." The officers had to tell him not to move.

David asked what he did wrong. The officer gently explained to the young man, "You got hit by a car. You're hurt. You're not in trouble."

He reassured him he would be ok, but he needed to hold still. David later said, "That may have made me give enough fight to just pull through and just have that hope to keep going."[1]

One of the officers held his legs so he wouldn't bleed out before the ambulance arrived.

An eyewitness described David's injuries as "horrific." He was "left for dead" by someone who was nowhere to be seen.

Debris was scattered along the road from the impact site to the place where the truck ultimately stopped. Emergency personnel found David's shredded wallet on North Crossover Road, as well as pieces from the scooter, two hats, both David's and Hailey's shoes, and a watch along the path. There was a trail that looked like skid marks the entire length that David and the scooter were dragged. Much of it was actually David's blood and flesh.

David arrived at the hospital before Hailey. His family was contacted. He was in surgery fighting for his life hours before officers came to Hailey's house. It took longer to figure out who she might be so her family could be notified.

David lost a lot of blood, and doctors did not expect him to survive the night. There was no way to save David's legs. The damage was too great. Both legs were amputated, one at the hip and the other above the knee. By the time he came out of surgery, Hailey was already gone.

It was not difficult for police officers to locate the truck involved in the hit-and-run. Blood stains and scrape marks from the scooter led right to the red Silverado, with the mangled scooter still under its front bumper. There was no sign of the driver.

The truck was registered to a woman who lived in the apartment complex. At 7:18 p.m., nineteen minutes after the truck hit Hailey, officers knocked on the door of the owner of the truck. She was not at home.

Her brother answered the door and confirmed to the officers that his sister owned the truck, but Sergio Rodriguez was the one who normally drove it. Police asked if they were married. Her brother said they were not but they had been together for three years.

Sergio was not home. No one had seen him since he left for work that morning. He told police he believed Sergio was with the truck, since his sister had left the house in her other vehicle about twenty minutes before.

He told the officers he did not have Sergio's phone number. He called his sister and told her there were police officers there who wanted to speak with her and Sergio. He asked her in Spanish, "Maria, esta nerviosa?" (*"Maria, are you nervous?"*) She was apparently nervous over the phone but told her brother she would come home right away.

She and her mother arrived home shortly after. She told the police she had not seen Sergio since she left for church with the rest of her family around 1:20 p.m. When they got back home at 4:30, he and the truck were gone. She said he often went out with friends to drink on weekends; however, no one at the apartment could tell the police any names or contact information for any of Sergio's friends. They did not speculate any locations where he might be.

She tried to call him multiple times while the police were there, but there was no answer.

Police asked her if she and Sergio were married. She responded they were not legally married but they had been together for three years.

The Silverado was impounded and towed away. Investigators photographed the truck and its contents. Photos showed a box of hypodermic needles in the glove box, a sweatshirt, a used condom and tissues in the back floorboard, and a cowboy hat on the dash. A charger and a bag of something tied up in a black trash bag were inside the console, and another black bag was in the floorboard of the passenger seat. An employee of the tow truck company told Kathy Hall a large quantity of marijuana and what appeared to be heroin was found in the truck.

Investigators searching the surrounding area found the ice chest with the beer hidden in the bushes. There was no sign of Rodriguez. No one knew where he was, or at least, no one admitted knowing his whereabouts.

Reporters showed up at the Halls' home by 5:30 a.m., hours after Hailey was pronounced dead. David was alive, but in critical condition. The perpetrator was nowhere to be found. News stations posted his name and photo, and asked for anyone having information about his location to call the police.

Sergio Rodriguez, age thirty-three, had a previous DUI on his record, and he was in the country illegally.

According to Arkansas state law, drivers involved in personal injury accidents must stay on the scene for at least thirty minutes, giving assistance or calling for help if needed. Had he simply stopped when he plowed into the scooter, perhaps Hailey would still be alive. If she had not been flung off of his truck at seventy-plus mph, maybe her injuries would have been survivable. Almost certainly David would not have lost his legs.

Sergio Rodriguez

Photo from Fayetteville AK Police Department Facebook page.

Sergio hid out for two days before turning himself in to the police. He showed up with his attorney at the Fayetteville Police Department about 3:00 p.m. on Tuesday, November 8. To date police do not know where he was between the time of the hit-and-run and his arrest.

His bail was set for twenty-five thousand dollars. The cash bond was posted, and somehow Sergio was back out on the street in a mere hour and forty-five minutes after surrendering to the police.

The day he turned himself in was Election Day 2016. When Kathy turned the TV on that evening, she saw election results scrolling across the bottom of the screen. That was not what made her freeze. Plastered on the screen was the face of the man who had taken her daughter's life. There were two big news stories that night in her region of Arkansas: Donald Trump's victory over Hillary Clinton in the Presidential election, and the arrest of Sergio Rodriguez for the hit-and-run that killed one victim and maimed another.

For Kathy, the election results were all but irrelevant. Any news of Trump winning the election paled in comparison to the fact that her baby girl was never coming home.

She later spoke of the election results in an interview and said she "didn't realize the significance then." How could she?

9 - Fighting for Justice

It took a few days for family and friends to get to Arkansas for Hailey's memorial service, which was scheduled for Tuesday, November 15. When her step-daughter came into town, she wanted to go to church with them the Sunday before the service. Kathy was angry with God for allowing her daughter to die, so she was not interested in going to church.

The church was being great to them, however, she said in hindsight. The pastor of the church the Halls attended would do Hailey's service. The church family stepped in to provide fried chicken with all the fixings for fifty people at the Hall home afterward.

Even so, it was hard for Kathy to bring herself to go to church on Sunday. She relented only for the sake of her step-daughter. Exhausted, Kathy fell asleep as soon as the service started. It was almost like she had passed out.

Jeff tried, unsuccessfully, to wake her up. "Baby, wake up. Baby, you gotta wake up."

She was finally in a place where she could relax for a few minutes. The supernatural peace of God came over her, and she was able to rest.

They got through the memorial service on Tuesday. Hailey's body was cremated immediately afterward. When Kathy got home, she lay down on her bed. After crying so much that week, a few tears quietly fell down her cheeks that evening. *I didn't know how to feel. Just complete shock, I guess. I hurt so bad inside.*

She noticed the mail sitting at the food of the bed. On top was an envelope from the prosecuting attorney's office. She opened it to find an introduction letter to the group—"Parents of Murdered Children."

"Until that very moment, I had never thought of myself as the parent of a murdered child." The thought took her breath.

It really did not look like an accident to her, but she had not thought of it in those terms before. The main detective in the case later told Kathy, "We've never really thought that this was an accident, but we couldn't get anybody to talk, and nobody would come forward with anything."

~ ~ ~

Hailey's life had been stolen from her, and her baby Brooklyn was foremost on everyone's thoughts. Her mother could no longer fight for her, but her family certainly could. They would never give up on her.

Kathy's attorney told her that, as Hailey's surviving minor child, Brooklyn was legally considered to be part of her estate. Hailey never lost her parental rights, and the state would have to let Brooklyn come home, he said. The courts could do nothing permanent with regard to Brooklyn until her mother's estate was settled, but she could return home in the interim.

Kathy filed a petition for guardianship of her granddaughter by the first week of December and requested an emergency hearing to bring her home. The Halls were more than capable financially to provide for Brooklyn's needs, and they very much wanted to bring her home with her remaining family.

The DHS case was opened against Hailey. Upon her death, any basis for the

DHS case no longer existed. There were no longer any legal grounds to keep Brooklyn in foster care—or so it should be if the issue were really that DHS was concerned about the child's safety in the care of her mother. This should have been a simple case to wrap up—return Brooklyn to her family and close the DHS case. That did not happen.

The circuit judge over Hailey's probate case stated that, since there was already a case involving Hailey and Brooklyn with DHS, the probate case and DHS case should be combined and sent to the presiding judge over the previously existing case. Thus, it all went back to Judge Stacey Zimmerman's courtroom.

The case was set for January 11, 2017. Meanwhile, DHS refused to allow any visits between Brooklyn and her extended family, and she remained in foster care.

~ ~ ~

On Christmas Day, less than two months after Hailey was gone, Kathy found a letter her daughter would had to have written the weekend she died. Kathy's feet were cold, so she went to grab a pair of wool socks from a bin. A crumpled piece of paper lay on top of the socks. It had not been there when Kathy cleaned out and reorganized the bin the Saturday before the wreck.

At first, Kathy thought it was a piece of trash. She almost threw it away, but something stopped her. She gasped as she recognized the handwriting on the paper. It was a letter addressed to her, from her daughter. Hailey had to have written it either Saturday night or Sunday before she left the house.

Mom,

im ok since i left
people will hurt you to get to me.
Know that I am telling you the truth. I Love you.
I promise ill be ok & ill make this right.
Trust no one but her.

—I love you.
Hailey King

Fresh waves of grief overwhelmed her as she crumbled to the ground sobbing. Kathy never figured out who Hailey was referring to when she said, "Trust no one but her."

~ ~ ~

Over the weeks and months following the crash, Kathy tried to reach out to David Gutierrez. She asked the prosecuting attorney's office to give his family her name and number. She had never heard Hailey mention David. Kathy asked many times to talk to David. The Victim Assistance Coordinator in the prosecutor's office repeatedly told her David was not ready to talk to her yet. This was not the case, as David told her later.

At the same time Kathy sought to connect with the other victim of the crime that took her daughter's life, David was being led to believe Hailey's family was angry with him and blamed him for Hailey's death. However, the Halls never blamed David. No matter what happened, they knew the only one to blame for the situation was the man who hit them with his truck and did not stop.

Kathy and David did not meet until much later—the day Sergio Rodriguez was finally sentenced for his crimes.

~ ~ ~

Meanwhile, on January 11, 2017, the Halls went to court. They expected to bring Brooklyn home. Several family members were present who were also willing and able to care for Brooklyn, including Hailey's aunt from Texas. She had already been approved to adopt through what is known as an interstate compact, a legal mechanism which allows children to be fostered or adopted across state lines.

DHS presented their side to the court, complete with their usual half-truths, false allegations, and misinformation which had typified Hailey's previous hearings. All the while, Kathy's attorney missed numerous opportunities to object and to correct inaccurate information. Each time Kathy asked him to speak up, he shushed her, telling her they had to wait their turn, and they would be next.

DHS informed the court Brooklyn was "adoptable." Several times throughout the hearing, Judge Zimmerman asked the social workers to clarify and reclarify this point. It was obviously important to this judge who presided over more DHS adoptions than any other judge in the state of Arkansas at the time.

Kathy wrote on a notepad to her attorney, "Why aren't you saying anything? She's not adoptable!"

Again, he whispered, "We'll be heard next."

Because of federal funding through the Adoption and Safe Families Act of 1997 (ASFA), billions of Title IV-E tax dollars are funneled to the states for adopting out children. This particular funding stream can only be accessed when foster children are adopted by strangers. It is not available when children are returned home or when children are adopted by family members. The state of Arkansas and Judge Zimmerman's court would pocket these funds if Brooklyn could be adopted by the foster parents, who were present at the hearing.[1]

Brooklyn's biological father was not in the picture. His relationship with Hailey ended before the baby was born, and he lived halfway across the country. After Hailey died, DHS approached him and led him to believe Brooklyn would be going to live with her grandparents. He trusted she would be in good hands with Hailey's family, so he relinquished his parental rights. Had he been fully informed of the intentions of DHS, he may well have made a different decision and fought for his daughter.

His parental rights were officially terminated at this hearing.

Kathy's attorney never addressed any of the issues he had filed on behalf of his client. He never spoke up in the courtroom. The family was not given any opportunity to address the court. Kathy felt invisible.

She thought they would have the opportunity to refute the social workers, but the only time she was addressed was when they asked her if she had Hailey's death certificate.

The court took a recess. The attorney assured Kathy they would have their turn after recess.

They did not. The bailiff came out and declared the hearing was over. "That's it. Court is over for the day. Go home."

Brooklyn remained in foster care, and her family was again denied the opportunity to have visits with her.

~ ~ ~

The Halls searched for a new attorney. Like many parents with children in Child Protective Services custody, they found it difficult to find an attorney with the courage to go up against DHS. They finally hired a new attorney in March and requested a new court date.

Fighting for Justice

On June 5, the new attorney hired by the Halls filed a petition with the court for Kathy and Jeff to adopt Brooklyn as her maternal grandparents.

~ ~ ~

While they fought to bring Hailey's child home, they found themselves fighting another battle they never thought they would have to fight. They believed when someone kills someone and leaves another person permanently maimed, the justice system would ensure the criminal is duly charged and punished. They did not realize that, in this arena as well as the family court system, they would have to contend for justice.

As a military family, the Halls believed in "truth, justice, and the American way." They believed the part of the Pledge of Allegiance which says, "with liberty and justice for all." Jeff had been willing to lay down his life for his country because of the ideals of the United States Constitution. He was injured in battle and received a purple heart for his sacrifice. Not in their wildest dreams did they ever fathom that justice would be such a difficult battle on the home front.

With their fight for Brooklyn against the powerful family/juvenile court system, they joined the ranks of countless veterans and service members who found that the biggest battle for justice happened, not overseas, but right here at home, in the courts, for their families. That is where they encounter things in the courtroom which stand in direct opposition to everything they once took an oath to defend. Disillusioned, the Halls determined to continue to stand for what they know is right.

The only charge against their daughter's killer originally was leaving the scene of an accident. The charge carried a maximum sentence of six years, but there was a possibility of just a six-month probation. For months it appeared he might literally be getting away with murder.

Kathy could not believe what she was seeing. She had made a solemn promise to her daughter as she lay lifeless in the hospital that she would fight for justice for Hailey and Brooklyn. That promise drove her.

For months she fought for stronger charges against Sergio Rodriguez. He was in the country illegally, but that part of the story seemed to be being swept under the rug.

Kathy later explained to radio talk show host Paul Harrell, "I understand car accidents happen, but when my daughter was on the hood of this man's truck for over 200 feet, and he never even slowed down, and he made the conscious decision to veer over into the other lane, hoping to knock her off—and he did—you know at that point he made that choice. As far as I am concerned, it was murder at that point."[2]

She talked to lawmakers. While fighting to get Brooklyn home on one front, Kathy did everything she could to ensure Brooklyn's mother's death was not ignored by the justice system. She went to the media and did several press conferences. She told the story of the illegal alien who killed her daughter to anyone who would listen. She asked what kind of soulless person would not stop and try to help the kids he hurt. Was the possibility of being deported worth the cost of human lives?

10 - Where is Justice?

One Friday evening in late July, Kathy sat down at her computer to unwind from everything going on in her world. Dinner was done. Jeff was out grocery shopping, and the house was quiet. She went to the foster parents' Facebook page, hoping to see a picture of Brooklyn. They were still waiting for a court date after filing to adopt her.

She had not seen her grandbaby since Hailey's death. Right there in the middle of the foster father's page was a beautiful photo of Brooklyn. Kathy's heart leaped with excitement. She missed her granddaughter terribly and was overjoyed to see her sweet, smiling face on her computer.

Brooklyn was surrounded by the foster family, but she looked adorable in her little pink boots. They knelt around a big sign, but the writing was too small to read. Kathy enlarged the picture to see what it said. She was completely unprepared for what she saw: "Today is my ADOPTION DAY! I'm officially Brooklyn [last name of fosters] <July 26, 2017>"

"No!!!" Kathy fell to the ground. *This can't be!* She screamed and wailed. She later described how she felt: "I wanted to die. It was just like Hailey just died all over again." She couldn't breathe. She yelled to the sky, "Hailey, I failed you!"

When Jeff came home, he found his wife on the ground, utterly distraught. He picked her up and held her close. He could not believe this was the way they had to find out Brooklyn got adopted two days before.

Hailey's rights to her child were never severed, but Judge Zimmerman and DHS adopted Brooklyn out to non-family members anyway.

A week after Kathy found the photo of Brooklyn's adoption, they were notified their own petition for adoption was denied. Judge Zimmerman stated in the court order that the petition was presented to the court on July 26, 2017. It was not. It couldn't have been. That was adoption day. Neither the Halls nor their attorney were notified of any hearing. Since the hearing did not occur, obviously no testimony could have been heard.

In the document, signed by Judge Zimmerman on July 31, 2017, the judge accused Kathy of being mentally unstable, "and is even more mentally unstable since her daughter (Hailey King, the mother of Brooklyn) was tragically killed in a scooter accident in November 2016."

A no-contact order was included in the document, which was never served to the Halls. It forbade both Kathy and Jeff to have any kind of contact with Brooklyn, in person, by phone, or by letter or electronic communication—essentially severing any kind of relationship between grandparents and grandchild.

The Halls and their attorney promptly filed a Motion to Reconsider and a legal brief on August 5. In their motion they asked that the judge's order be "set aside to prevent the miscarriage of justice."

The motion "suggested that the Court is not in a position to make this determination based upon an apparent recollection from November 2016, when Kathryn Hall's daughter was killed, when it is now August 2017, and the Court has made its decision without a hearing or testimony."

Judge Zimmerman is not a medical professional. Judges are not qualified to make a determination that someone is mentally unstable, but it is not uncommon for social workers and judges in family court situations to "diagnose" parents with various mental maladies and conditions, despite their lack of medical training and the illegality of their making such diagnoses.

Kathy has never been diagnosed with mental instability or any other mental disorder. She later said sarcastically in a blog talk interview, "I guess it made me mentally unstable to fight for my child and my grandchild."[1]

After Judge Zimmerman's "diagnosis," Kathy sought out a grief counselor to help her process her daughter's death. She asked him if he thought she was mentally unstable. "On the contrary," he said. She was an inspiration. In fact, he invited Kathy to speak about her story at an event at one of the largest churches in the area.

The court never answered the Halls' petition. Much later, on March 9, 2018, Judge Zimmerman filed an order to dismiss the petition, stating (incorrectly) that the issue was addressed on July 26, 2017—adoption day, a day on which there was no hearing regarding or involving the Halls.

~ ~ ~

Almost a year after Hailey was killed, prosecutors from the State of Arkansas filed charges against Sergio Rodriguez. On September 6, 2017, Sergio Rodriguez was charged with three criminal counts, with a possibility of fifty-eight years of prison:

1. Murder in the Second Degree—Class A Felony—for Hailey's death.
2. Battery in the First Degree—Class B Felony—for David's injuries.
3. Leaving the Scene of an Accident—Class D Felony.

His trial was set for January 22, 2018. He hired attorney Kim Webber for a twenty-thousand dollar retainer fee, and paid twelve thousand dollars for his expert witnesses.

~ ~ ~

Meanwhile, disturbing rumors circulated about the man who had killed Hailey and maimed David—that he was part of a Mexican cartel. The Halls had no way of knowing whether or not this was true, but they were scared. Kathy had roots in Colorado, and she and Jeff agreed it was time to move back. In early November, they packed up two moving trucks and relocated to the Colorado mountains. There they escaped the constant reminders of their pain in Arkansas, but the memories were never far away.

In December, a month before Sergio's scheduled trial, he was permitted to marry the woman he had been living with, thus making him a "permanent legal resident."

The state brought in a new prosecutor on the case, and the trial was postponed. This would be the third prosecutor since the crash.

~ ~ ~

One quiet afternoon that winter, Kathy looked into a box of Hailey's things, untouched since the move. She found her daughter's Bible. As she flipped through the pages, she saw where Hailey wrote that she accepted Jesus as her Savior on July 22, 2016. She read through all of the Scripture verses that Hailey had underlined, and she talked to God. *I don't understand. Why was it so important for Hailey to underline these specific things? What was going on in her head? What was she going through?*

As she continued to read the passages, a sense of peace descended upon her like a warm, comforting blanket. God did not save Hailey when Kathy was in the hospital room crying out to Him. She was already gone, but she did not suffer. Kathy realized then that God stopped the suffering for Hailey, and she made her peace with Him.

~ ~ ~

She would need every ounce of God's strength she could get. Not long after she found Hailey's Bible, the new prosecutor negotiated a plea deal with Sergio Rodriguez and his attorney in early April, against vehement opposition from the victims and families. The prosecutor backed off from charging him with murder.

He would be sentenced to no more than twenty years in prison if he decided to plead guilty to the crimes of Manslaughter, Battery in the Second Degree, and Leaving the Scene of an Accident Involving Personal Injury or Death. There were no consequences for him being in the country illegally and committing his crimes. There were no consequences for other issues such as driving without a license, or for the vehicle having inadequate insurance.

He took the deal on April 9, 2018.

11 - Soulless Eyes

Kathy and David each finalized their Victim Impact Statements, to be read to the court before Sergio was sentenced. They had been thinking about what to say and preparing them for months. The statements were their chance for the judge to hear how Sergio Rodriguez's crimes impacted them emotionally and physically and changed their lives.

The sentencing hearing took place two days after Rodriguez took the plea deal. When Kathy arrived at the Washington County courthouse before the hearing began, an attendant directed her to the prosecuting attorney's office. She walked into the office and saw a young Hispanic man in a wheelchair who was missing his legs. It did not take a rocket scientist to figure out this had to be David Gutierrez.

She ignored the awkward glances of the Victim Assistance Coordinator who was leaning over by David's wheelchair. Kathy stuck her hand out and said, "Hi, David. I'm Kathy, Hailey's mom."

It felt surreal. After all this time of being kept apart, they were finally able to meet. They chatted a few minutes before it was time to go to the courtroom.

Kathy met Jeff and Hailey's father in the courtroom. David's mother and sister joined him. The other side of the courtroom was filled with people who came to support Rodriguez.

After he was seated on the bench behind Kathy, David leaned over and whispered, "Would you like to talk after court?"

"I would love that."

The media recorded the proceedings from behind a glass window. They could see, but not hear, what happened in the courtroom.

The prosecutor spoke first, informing the court that Sergio Rodriguez pleaded guilty to the charges as amended. There were going to be two Victim Impact Statements read to the court before sentencing.

Kathy spoke first. Her heart raced and her voice shook as she read the statement she had prepared. By the time she finished, she was sobbing.

My name is Kathryn. I am the mother of Hailey King. My daughter was the youngest of four children. She was my miracle baby being born prematurely. We did not know if she'd survive. Hailey was rushed to Saint Luke's hospital right after her birth to an ICU unit. As soon as I could, I left the hospital to be with her and her dad. That's where I held my beautiful baby girl for the first time.

I never dreamed I would have to also say goodbye to her so early in an ICU unit. Hailey was a fighter from her very first breath. At five months she once again was in ICU—this time with RSV. I remember once being so scared I would lose her, I would crawl inside the oxygen tent at night to sleep next to her.

She started softball at age five, and she played until she died. She was the happiest little girl. She was always laughing to the point we used to have to tell her, "It's not funny." My little girl did not cry; instead she laughed with them. When I asked her why, she told me then she didn't let them see her cry. She would rather make them her friend. Hailey tried to find the best in everyone no matter what. I recently ran across a post she wrote about herself that describes her perfectly. Every bit of what she wrote was her until the moment she died.

"I am Hailey Cyell King. I'm a teenager who loves easy, loves those who don't deserve it, and laughs to try not to cry. I'm Hailey Cyell King. I'm not perfect, but I don't care about the drama, and I will follow my dreams."

And that is who Hailey was.

On November 6, 2016, I lived every parent's worst nightmare. It started with the sirens I heard about a block away from my home. I felt a knot in the pit of my stomach as there were more sirens. Hailey had missed dinner and was not answering her phone. About four hours later, there was a knock on the door. I knew by the look on the detectives' faces it was not good. I felt frozen and scared to ask. When I was told that I needed to verify it was Hailey, to describe marks on her body until they were satisfied it was her. At that point they asked me to go with them to the hospital.

I spent the next hour and forty-five minutes watching the life leave my child's eyes, and there was nothing I could do to help her. Nothing! Life support was not even enough to keep her breathing. When her heart stopped for the last time, I felt as if the walls were closing in around me and I could not breathe. All I could think was I wanted to crawl back into that baby bed and listen to her breathe.

I do not remember running out of the hospital or how I ended up on the ground yelling and cursing God, then trying to bargain with Him to take my life instead of hers. But there I was. All I wanted was to go back in to that room and hear her laugh. That laugh that was so contagious. That laugh that I can still hear today in my head and in my heart.

None of Hailey's brothers or sister were able to make it to the hospital in time to say goodbye. My family fell apart after her death. There was no one to blame because the person responsible could not be found for days….

I have very few memories of the next year following her death. The memories I do have are of the nightmares of my child being hit on the back of that scooter, being hit by everything from a boulder to a train, while I could do nothing but watch over and over again. When I close my eyes, I see her once again with her eyes open and the life draining out of them.

Four months after her death, my husband finally moved us out of Fayetteville. I could not leave my home without seeing where my child landed in the street. Trying to leave would send me into a panic, which I had never before experienced. Then panic would set in that she would come home and I wouldn't be there. Although the expense was more than we could afford, we had to move.

A knock at the door at night still brings me to my knees. I cannot be in a room or area where I feel confined....

Hailey was our ray of sunshine for eighteen short years until one man's choice violently took her life away, not only from me but from her two-year-old baby girl that will now grow up with no memories of her mommy or know how much her mother loved and adored her. Our family has lost a piece of our stitching that held us together and can never be mended.

It has taken me some time to realize that there will never be justice for Hailey's life being taken, especially not today. For the first time since her death, I think we the family of Hailey King agree on something. For the last seventeen months, we have had to live without Hailey, knowing this man spent less than two hours in jail and was released to go home to his child.

One week after we said goodbye to my child, he was posing for Thanksgiving photos with his child. My child was dead due to his actions, and it was my birthday. A few months ago I received a message on Facebook from a family member of the defendant saying that he was not who I thought he was, and that he would never hurt anyone.

I did not respond to the message until now. No, I do not know him, but what I do know is this: He did hurt somebody and he did kill my child. So I know more than I ever wanted or wished to know about him. As much as I hope he never forgets my child's name or her face, we are stuck never forgetting his.

I have thought about this day for seventeen long months and what I would say. I have tried to find it in my heart to forgive, but I cannot. The actions this man took after hitting my daughter and never stopping or trying to get any help for either of the victims is something I cannot ever imagine doing even to a wild animal. He thought about his self first and foremost, and this I cannot now or ever understand. Thank you.

She walked back to her seat, her face wet with tears. As she glanced over at Sergio Rodriguez, their eyes locked. What she saw shook her to her core. "His eyes were soulless. There was absolutely no remorse."

12 - "No Escape from This Nightmare"

It was David's turn to speak next. He steeled himself, and his voice rose clear and strong as he addressed the courtroom:

It is only through sheer empirical and anecdotal evidence by which I am able to testify of the consequences and actions took by Mr. Rodriguez on the fateful day he committed his crime. The unfolding of events has affected me, and the nature is three-fold, concerning my mind, body, and spirit.

I myself am living, physical evidence to what had occurred, for all those that look at me now are able to see the last repercussions I deal with on a day-to-day basis. Basic activities and daily living such as communing, doing laundry, eating, and bowel movements are now at least twice more demanding and time consuming. Not only that, but due to the state of my mobility, I am now at twice the risk for heart disease, and prone to obesity.

There have also been episodes where I wake up in the middle of the night to my lower extremities convulsing in a sporadic manner which may be caused by the phantom pains that have been incorporated into my daily life. All day the stress my body is put under has a direct influence to my behaviors and psyche that manifests itself in various ways: anxiety, despair, isolation, depression, frustration, anguish, and fear are some things that I continue to cope with every day.

It's always a struggle to motivate myself to get up every morning. The monotony of sitting for countless hours implements a sensation of imprisonment within my own body, due to the restrictions I have, being bound to a wheelchair. So it's no wonder why I wish I could sleep my days away and dream.

But even if I could, my dreams have turned into nightmares. Sometimes there is no escape from this reality, even in my own dreams. There have been many instances now where I am dreaming and I realize I am walking. Upon the realization, I recognize I am dreaming, and reality begins to set in—the outcome being is, the dream turns violent, and somehow my legs are maimed to the point I can't walk any more, or I suddenly lose the strength in my legs and they gave out beneath me. Either way I end up spending the rest of the dream trying to find a way to walk, or just lay there on the floor, wallowing in sorrow, anger, and discontent.

It doesn't matter where I go, because my spirit always seems to be in a state of perpetual affliction in one form or another. I can't even take a stroll on the sidewalk by myself any more without being paranoid that cars will come and hit me from behind. Constantly when I'm out and about, I find myself looking over my shoulders. It's a preventative measure I need to take in order to reassure myself I am safe. But even there, the fear never leaves. For the rest of my life, I will drag around these insecurities just like he dragged me around the block.

The judge might be able to give him a sentence, but he has sentenced me to a life without legs. He might be going to prison, but I will be incarcerated in my own body for life, which is a result of him deciding not to stop.

From that moment on, he has done nothing but think of himself, because it's obvious by his actions he didn't think about me or Hailey when he hit us. Based on that decision, it confers the accident into a crime, thus forever punishing two youth for a crime they did not commit.

David spoke a few words in Spanish, then continued in English:

To translate on my own behalf, I said—the last thing I want to say is that I have forgiven him. If he does not repent, the revenge will be God's, not mine. Since my accident, I took it upon myself to live primarily for the goal to find God's purpose that He has for me and enjoy life to the fullest for Hailey's sake, and lastly to live it myself.

I would like to thank those that took the time I took to testify. Thanks again to you all.

With that, he wheeled back to the bench to join his family. The mood in the room was somber after his dramatic testimony. Kathy reached her hand back and squeezed his shoulder. Without a word between them, they each knew how the other felt, though they never met before that day.

Sergio Rodriguez and his attorney Kimberly Weber were sworn in. Judge Mark Lindsay addressed Rodriguez in reference to a previous conversation, acknowledging the fact that the state had the evidence to prove his crimes. "Do you remember that, after hearing an account of the proof that the state intended to put on, you told me that that was true, in other words, that they could prove what they said they were going to prove?"

His attorney answered for him. "Yes, your honor."

His guilty plea on all counts was reaffirmed, and the judge stated that he would be provided with copies of his victims' impact statements.

Weber muttered the obligatory statement that her client was "very remorseful" for the "horrible tragedy."

To which, Judge Lindsay addressed Sergio. "Does Mr. Rodriguez have anything to say?" He did not.

The judge said he felt obligated to say a few words after listening to Kathy's and

David's testimonies of how Sergio's crimes impacted them. He acknowledged the state had no power to make the victims whole. Nothing anyone could do would give Kathy back her daughter or give David back his legs. The only thing the state could do was punish the offender and hope for the rehabilitation of the criminal.

He pronounced the sentence that the prosecutor and Sergio Rodriguez agreed to:

— 120 months (10 years) for the crime of Manslaughter in Hailey's death,

— 60 months (5 years) for the crime of Battery in the Second degree for David's legs, and

— 24 months (2 years) for the crime of Leaving the Scene of an Accident Involving Personal Injury and Death.

The sentences were to be served consecutively, for a total of 204 months (17 years). When he is released from prison, he will be required to pay thirty dollars in booking and administrative fees and a two-hundred fifty-dollar fee for a DNA sample.

There would be no restitution paid to the families he harmed. The prosecutors' office previously told Kathy that the courts there never did that. There is a place for it on the Sentencing Form, but it was not, they informed Kathy, the practice to request restitution for victims in Washington County, Arkansas.

Much of the medical bills and funeral costs had to be borne by the families, because the truck was underinsured. Hailey's medical bills were forty-eight thousand dollars, but the truck's insurance only covered twenty-five thousand of those costs. David had to get attorneys to help him collect insurance from the crash. They ultimately collected twenty-five thousand dollars from the liability insurance, but the attorneys took a third, leaving the remaining sixteen and a half thousand dollars to cover his medical bills and expenses incurred in adapting to a life without legs.

The sentence would begin, the judge said, when a bed became available at the Arkansas Department of Corrections.

Weber requested her client be given two weeks to get his affairs in order. (Up until this point, Sergio had spent a total of less than two hours in jail. He had been free on his twenty-five thousand dollar bond for the seventeen months since his arrest.) She stated he was not a flight risk.

Wait a minute, Kathy's mind reeled. *He's not from the U.S. He's illegal. He's not a flight risk? Did he pull over when he hit my daughter and stay there and do the right thing, or did he flee until he was found? He's not a flight risk?*

The judge looked to the prosecutor. "What does the state say?"

"The state does not object."

Up until this point, Kathy, David, and their respective families watched in stunned silence.

Kathy could not sit back another minute. She cried out, "What?!"

Other voices clamored, and David's voice rang out over the dismay of the crowd. "Come on!"

Another woman pleaded, "He's been out for seventeen months—"

"He's had seventeen months, but my child is dead!"

It looked like the judge was about to say something. Kathy could swear she knew what he was about to say, and she looked him in the eye, daring him to throw her in jail for contempt while the man who murdered her daughter was about to be given another two weeks of freedom before going to jail.

At that moment the lady recording the proceedings for the court made a gesture to him and said something Kathy could not hear. She believed the woman was reminding him the press was present on the other side of the window, recording everything.

The judge addressed the crowd in the room. "Ladies and gentlemen, this proceeding is open to the public, but if there are any more outbursts, people may have to be asked to leave.

"Now let's see. First of all, this is something that is done as much for the sheriff's detention center as it is a defendant. Our judges—if any of you read the newspaper, you will know that Washington County Detention Center is overcrowded, and beds do not become available immediately in the Department of Corrections, and that is just a fact of life. So this was something that was done for the benefit of the Detention Center, and it is done just as a matter of policy in every case where the state does not object."

He then instructed the attorneys to prepare an order for Sergio to turn himself in to the police at 8:00 a.m. on April 25.

Kathy stormed out of the courtroom, kicking open the door.

David joined her a few minutes later in the hall. "Oh, my God. I cannot believe that. It was so obvious that he was going to put you in contempt of court and have you taken to jail."

"Yeah, I know. That's why I stared him down like, 'I dare you.' Go ahead and say you don't have room for a murderer, but you were going to put a mother who just lost her child in jail for contempt for speaking out."

Just then her ex-husband came up to them. "He was going to put you in jail for contempt. You've got bigger balls than I ever had, because I can't believe that just happened."

"I knew what he was going to say. It was so obvious."

~ ~ ~

When Sergio Rodriguez reported to the police department two weeks later, he was taken to a low-security prison farm for non-violent offenders. Kathy was furious. She went to *Fox News* and told the story about the illegal alien who took her daughter's life and left a young man without his legs. Shortly after, she learned he was sent to a medium security prison.

It seemed to the victims' families there were people in the justice system who bent over backwards for Sergio Rodriguez and other people who were in the country illegally who commit crimes.

13 - "You Have Help Now"

Kathy had made a promise to her daughter that she would never give up on getting justice for her family. Her granddaughter was not home. She never stopped trying to get people to listen to her about the corruption her family experienced at the hands of the Child Protective System and the family courts, but both legislators and the media seemed to be tone deaf to her pleas.

On the other hand, her daughter's killer was finally in prison. It had been a hard fight to see him charged with Hailey's death and the loss of David's legs in the callous hit-and-run. Even then, the charges were not enough. He had gotten off too lightly. Nothing would bring her precious baby girl back to her.

Donald J. Trump was in the White House, and a few legislators and media people were more open to discussing the illegal immigration issue than they were the CPS issue. Though it was a politically controversial issue, the press gave airtime to the stories Kathy brought to them of Rodriguez seeming to get away with murder as an illegal alien. That part of Kathy's story was easier to get people to listen to because the crisis at the border was a hot, trending issue in the news at the time.

Kathy's passionate fight to see Hailey's killer brought to justice caught the attention of another justice warrior. Mary Ann Mendoza founded Angel Families, a group of Americans brought together by the same heartbreaking tragedy. Each member has someone in their family who was killed by an illegal. Mary Ann's son, Sgt. Brandon Mendoza of the Mesa Arizona police department, was killed in 2014 by a habitual criminal who was in the United States illegally.

A friend had already suggested to Kathy that she contact the group, but before she decided to make the call, Mary Ann reached out to her, shortly after the sentencing of Sergio Rodriguez. She wanted Kathy to come on board with Angel Families. The group's mission was to tell their stories and work toward changing laws and policies that have led to the senseless deaths of American citizens at the hands of illegals. Because Kathy had already been speaking to media and lawmakers, Mary Ann was confident Kathy's voice would be a welcome addition to help them get their message heard.

Kathy agreed to join them. That decision launched her onto a much larger platform than she had before, and she plunged in wholeheartedly—traveling, speaking at rallies, and doing media interviews, focused on the problems of people coming into the country illegally.

She heard the stories of other Angel Families, and learned about policies and statistics. She learned that, in Mexico, it is not illegal to leave the scene of an accident,[1] even if there are injuries or fatalities involved.

~ ~ ~

Still, the grief of missing Hailey and Brooklyn never left. The part of her story about CPS taking Brooklyn and adopting her out to strangers was not something people seemed interested in hearing. The prevailing mentality was that, if a child was taken by CPS or DHS, "then surely there must be a reason." Over and over she heard, "They don't take children for no reason," or "Your daughter must have done something wrong." Those were the kind of responses she, and many other parents, typically got whenever they tried to talk about children being wrongfully removed by CPS.

How dare she criticize foster care or adoption? Foster parents and adoptive parents are practically saints, taking in those poor, neglected, abused children no one else wants—or at least that is the way it is presented to the public. Mainstream media did not want to touch that part of Kathy's story with a ten-foot pole.

Even though there was clearly fraud involved in DHS keeping Brooklyn in their custody and adopting her out, neither lawyers nor legislators seemed to want to listen, much less do anything about it.

It was easy for Kathy to fall into despair. The thought of possibly never seeing Brooklyn again was more than she could bear. She had promised Hailey—*promised* her—she would bring Brooklyn home. But she could not even get a single legislator to do more than patronizingly pat her on her head and send her on her way with broken promises that they would "look into it." They never did.

Was it any wonder then that she didn't want to hear from her friend Sam again when he said she should reach out to Senator Linda Collins-Smith? How different could she be from all the other Senators and Congressmen she had already talked to?

But Linda WAS different. Just when Kathy had given up all hope that anyone in the legislature would ever be willing to look into DHS, Linda responded to Kathy's desperate tweet on May 29, 2018, and said, "You have it [help] now," just over a month after Sergio was finally taken to prison.

Kathy knew nothing of Linda's history or political career before they talked on the phone that day. Linda told Kathy she had been looking into problems with DHS in the state of Arkansas for quite some time already, and she was very interested in checking into Kathy's story. From the beginning of their relationship, Child Protective Services concerns were every bit as big a part of Kathy and Linda's conversations as the fact that Hailey had been killed by an illegal.

Linda Collins-Smith had a reputation for being a passionate patriot and tenacious advocate for conservative values. She was pro-life, pro-family, and pro-Constitution. Not only did she identify as a Christian, she lived a life which backed it up.

Before she entered politics, she was a successful businesswoman and real estate agent. The mother of two was elected to the Arkansas House of Representatives, District 80, in November 2010. Linda quickly established herself as one of the most conservative Democrats in the Arkansas legislature.

She believed legislators work for the people, not the other way around. By eight months into her term, she realized her values more closely aligned with the Republican Party than the Democrats. In a press conference on August 10, 2011, she announced she was switching parties. She had become involved in politics in order to represent the common man. The people who elected her "want[ed] and deserve[d] elected officials who will stand for what is right, who will say what they mean and do what they say."[2] Yet, she found the party she grew up in was at the point where it "tolerates no independent thinking within its ranks," she said. "I know, because I lived it."

She was still the same person she was when the people of her district elected her, and she committed to continue to work for the "hard-working common sense people" of her state, vowing to work "side-by-side with [them] to bring our state government back to the values of the good and decent people of Arkansas."[3]

When the time came for her to run for reelection, the lines of her district had been redrawn, putting her in the same district as another Republican woman, Representative Lori Benedict. Linda chose to run for the Senate instead, in the newly-drawn Senate District 19. She was defeated in 2012, but won the seat in the November 2014 election.

In her position as a Senator, she was involved in meetings with the Joint Performance Review Committee where she joined chair Senator Alan Clark and others in asking hard questions of DHS. Numerous cases of the state taking children from families had come to the attention of the legislators on the committee, involving children who should not have been removed but were taken anyway. She questioned DHS as to why this was happening. She learned that case workers often entered "true findings" in cases where the allegations against the parents were not true,[4] and she wanted to know why.

The senator was part of hearings addressing the departments' abuse of power in cases such as that of minister Hal Stanley and his wife Michelle. Their seven homeschooled children were seized by DHS on the night of January 12, 2015 (ten months before Brooklyn was taken from Hailey). Linda heard Rev. Stanley testify how his children were taken by social workers accompanied by armed police officers, all based on false allegations. The children were separated, placed into separate foster homes, and enrolled into public school while their parents fought for their freedom.[5]

The committee requested documents from DHS as a part of their investigation, but the agency stonewalled the committee for months, obliging only when the legislature threatened to withhold their funding. Even when DHS finally turned over their documents on the case, they withheld an internal email sent by a supervisor to other DHS workers the very day after the Stanley children were taken. When it surfaced in October of 2016, a year and a half later, Senator Alan Clark called the email the "smoking gun" in a cover-up by DHS to hide the fact that the state had no legitimate reason to seize the children, and they knew it from the very beginning.

In the email, the DHS worker wrote, "From reports, the search warrant did not find anything that would constitute the children being severely maltreated. It appears to me that the only thing this family has done is not conform to modern society and how certain government officials feel they should be living."[6]

After this email was brought up in a committee meeting, "there was an attempt to shut down the meeting and then the committee itself."[7] Both Senators Alan Clark and Linda Collins-Smith were replaced on the committee the next session.

Around the same time the whistleblower revealed the email, an analysis was released by a consulting firm contracted by DHS which concluded that, over a recent 14-month period, "at least 300 child removals may have been unnecessary, contributing to a 30-percent increase in children entering the foster system from January 2015 to the end of" May 2016.[8]

If this was what a firm contracted with the agency found, who knows how many more children were taken from their families who should not have been? What would an analysis find if conducted by a third party without such a conflict of interest?

By the time Senator Linda Collins-Smith saw Kathy Hall's desperate post on Twitter, she was already well aware that there were serious problems with DHS and CPS, not only in Arkansas, but throughout the United States.

As Linda talked with Kathy the night of May 29, 2018, she knew there was good reason to look into Hailey's story. She had seen so much already, but neither Linda nor Kathy had any clue at the time how much deeper they would be going down the rabbit hole over the coming year.

Right away the two became close friends and confidantes. They started out talking about once a week or so. It wasn't long before they were calling each other almost every day.

Days before the tweet brought the two friends together, Linda lost her reelection bid in the primary on May 22, 2018, to James Sturch. However, she would remain in the legislature until the next January. She vowed to Kathy she would work with her to accomplish as much as possible by the end of her term.

As Kathy quickly learned, these were not empty words. Linda set out with impassioned determination to change things so that no families in the future would have to go through the heartache and injustice that Kathy and her family experienced.

Kathy posted a message on June 13 to Linda's Twitter page in support of her, despite her losing the election. "We lost a great Senator come January. I truly hope you are not done."

Linda responded within the hour, publicly addressing the fraud she saw in her state. "Thank you. I am making sure I continue to do my job & haven't slept much since fraud issues, corruption, neglect in cases & DHS, medicaid abuse cases, have ramped up, collusion, to the top gov officials ..see where it ends..who spews First get Best deal! #arkleg #fed."

14 - Secrets

"Though she be but little, she is fierce." – William Shakespeare

Though their conversations began with discussions of Brooklyn being taken by DHS, it was not long before they delved into the immigration issue. Linda immediately dug into investigating exactly what had happened to Kathy's family and what the legislature could do about it. Her investigation was two-pronged—illegal immigration and Child Protective Services.

As soon as Linda learned about Kathy's story, she asked DHS and the Washington County Court for the case files regarding Brooklyn. Initially they told her the files had been misplaced. However, every time after that when the Senator tried to get the files, there was one excuse or another why they could not get the files to her.

In her role as a legislator, she was supposed to be able to access the files as part of investigations into cases as she served her constituents. As Senator Alan Clark found previously in 2015-16 when he requested documents on the Hal Stanley family case, DHS was not forthcoming with the files. Like Senator Clark, Senator Collins-Smith faced an uphill battle in simply trying to get at the truth from DHS.

It was increasingly clear to her that there were failures in all three branches of government which allowed this kind of injustice to occur—legislative, judicial, and executive. Legislatively, laws were inadequate or had loopholes which were able to be exploited. Judicially, there were cavernous gaps in judicial consistency and accountability. The Child Protective Services agency, Arkansas' DHS, fell under the executive branch, where it was painfully obvious to Linda that there was a substantial overreach of power by those involved in the department.

Washington County, the county where Hailey's baby was taken and adopted out to strangers, had a huge Juvenile Justice Center, which housed the courthouse dealing with the juvenile and family court cases. Judge Stacey Zimmerman presides over the court—a court which oversees far more adoption cases than any other county in the entire state of Arkansas. Her county has twice as many children in foster care as other counties with similar demographics and population.

Once Kathy's family fell victim to Zimmerman's court, she found other families in Washington County with similar stories of unjustly taken children. As she and Linda continued to search, they realized these stories were not unique to Arkansas. They were happening, unchecked, all over the United States.

In fact, according to the latest AFCARS report from the U.S. Department of Health and Human Services, less than sixteen percent of children CPS takes from their families across the United States are taken for reasons of any kind of abuse.[1] Most children are removed from their homes under the nebulously-defined allegation of "neglect," which can be construed as just about anything a social worker wants it to be. While neglect has been used to rescue children from situations of extreme danger and neglect, involving cases where there is ample evidence to charge parents criminally, children have been seized from loving families for "neglect" involving dirty dishes in the sink, goldfish crackers on the carpet in front of the TV, or cases like Hailey's, where the parent left a child in the safe care of loving grandparents while going out of town for a weekend.

Even so, fewer than eighteen percent of all allegations against parents are "substantiated," which, according to the annual *Child Maltreatment Report* published by the U.S. Department of Health and Human Services, means "the allegation of maltreatment or risk of maltreatment is supported or founded by state law or policy." Most of the allegations are unsubstantiated.[2]

As hundreds of thousands of parents have learned, social workers and family/juvenile courts can, and do, substantiate accusations against them based on hearsay, opinion, or outright lies, while ignoring evidence which exonerates the parents. The widespread belief by social workers that this is acceptable practice was addressed in the infamous "Right to Lie" case of Preslie Hardwick v. Marcia Vreeken in 2016. Lawyers for Orange County, California, argued in front of the 9th Circuit Court of Appeals that there is no Constitutional grounds forbidding social workers to commit perjury in order to take children from their parents. The panel of justices disagreed, and the social workers lost their case for immunity.[3] Nonetheless, the practice continues unabated throughout Child Protective agencies across the nation.

Representative Kelly Townsend (later Senator) attempted to address these failures of the Child Protective System in her state of Arizona in 2017 by introducing legislation which would have prohibited Child Protective Services workers from influencing the outcome of a case by:

- Lying about a matter
- Withholding material information
- Fabricating evidence; or
- Failing to disclose known exculpatory evidence.[4]

Unfortunately, this effort was defeated by the Arizona legislature. Townsend was able, however, to secure an amendment to SB1003 which prohibits social workers and law enforcement from taking a child from their school or home unless a warrant is obtained, per the 4th Amendment of the U.S. Constitution, or exigent circumstances exist.

Just as it was when social workers seized Brooklyn from Kathy, the 4th amendment is routinely ignored in child welfare cases all around the nation. Social workers frequently cite exigent circumstances in order to take a child without a warrant. Townsend's amendment reiterates that exigent circumstances are narrowly defined as those emergency circumstances in which a child is in imminent danger of harm in the time it would take to obtain a court order. "Exigent circumstances" was never intended to be something written on a whim in order to seize a child when it is inconvenient to contact a judge or when they are knowingly attempting to circumvent the expectation that they have actual evidential grounds to intervene.

Several legislators in Arkansas recognized there were big problems with CPS and the courts which facilitate the transfer of children from one household to another. A great deal of money was changing hands on the backs of these children. Some lawmakers, including Senator Linda Collins-Smith, looked into how and why that happened as well as ways they could protect families in their state from the overreach of power they were seeing happen by DHS.

There are laws on both the federal level and the state level which contribute to the problem. Because Linda was a Senator in the State of Arkansas government, it was on the state level she believed she could best work to make a difference. By the time she learned of Kathy Hall's story, Linda had already been hard at work and digging deep.

Through their regular phone conversations, Linda and Kathy's friendship quickly grew beyond a strictly professional relationship. The two shared information they were learning as they researched, and they shared their hearts. The stories were gut-wrenching. If Kathy had not seen it happen to her own family, she would have had a hard time believing what she was seeing. Linda watched stories play out in real time as she examined the documentation provided by parents.

Families were being ripped apart without any logical justification, and for too many of them, justice was elusive. Loopholes were being exploited, and the public remained largely ignorant of what was really happening to foster children. It was hard to process, and the two friends bonded over their common determination to find ways to expose and end the corruption.

Kathy's pain was apparent, but the more they talked, she realized something more must be going on with her legislative friend. Every now and then, there was a comment, a tone, or a sigh from Linda that caused Kathy to wonder what was going on beneath the surface. Was there something deeper which caused Linda to identify with the plight of the abused? Is that why she fought so hard for them?

Linda had filed for divorce from her husband in November of 2017. She did not speak of him much at first. Kathy got the sense there was more going on than her friend let on, but she didn't push her to talk about it.

Not long after, the subject came up in conversation. The more Linda talked, the more she poured out her heart to Kathy.

Her soon-to-be ex-husband was a respected judge in the community. He served the city of Pocahontas and Randolph County as a municipal judge for nine years before being appointed by Governor Mike Huckabee as Circuit Judge for Arkansas' Third Judicial Circuit in March 2001. He was elected and re-elected since that time for the same seat. His jurisdiction covered four counties—Jackson, Lawrence, Randolph, and Sharp Counties. Judge Smith presided primarily over criminal and civil cases as well as probate and domestic relations cases. He also heard some juvenile cases, including DHS and adoption cases.

In such a position, he had the opportunity to make a powerful positive impact on the lives of those he served.

He presented an altogether different persona to his wife when they were alone. Most people did not realize it, Linda confided to Kathy, but they had been separated for a couple of years. In private, he was not the man she thought she married. The abuse started only a year after they were married and continued over the years. Linda was embarrassed and humiliated, so she stayed silent for many years.

She had a scar under her arm because he pushed her through a window. Her husband refused to take her to the hospital until someone else came in the room and saw all the blood.

That was not the worst of it, by far.

Linda told Kathy a horrifying story that happened in the early 2000s. She had numerous health issues over the past few years and had been getting sicker and sicker, but doctors could not figure out what it was. She went to the hospital, but the doctors there were just as clueless.

She got to the point of being essentially bedridden, with no energy to do anything.

Finally, she went to a hospital in Memphis, Tennessee. Because she was a real estate agent who went into a lot of houses and also oversaw some houses being renovated, she thought there was a possibility of lead poisoning. The doctor checked for lead, but he also tested for other heavy metals.

Her husband was with her, sitting in a chair by her bed in the hospital room, when a doctor came into the room accompanied by a police officer.

"You've been poisoned," the doctor said. "Somebody has been poisoning you."

Linda told Kathy her husband simply looked at the ground and refused to look up.

The officer gently explained, "Ma'am, somebody is trying to kill you. The doctor says you have mercury poisoning."

Linda tried to hide her shock. It was not lead poisoning, easily explained by her involvement with old houses. Instead, it was something much worse.

"Since nobody else in your house has any signs of being sick," the officer continued, "it is obvious you're the target."

Everyone in the room, Linda said, looked at Phil. It was clear the officer was there to arrest her husband, but Linda did not respond. She did not know what to say. Her husband never said a word.

Without further evidence or an admission of guilt, they let it drop.

Still, Linda stayed in the marriage and tried to keep going, pouring herself into her work, trying to make a difference for other people. As hurt as she was, she endeavored to be a good wife, suffering in silence—until something happened that she could not ignore. Linda told Kathy she filed for divorce right after making a shocking discovery.

She had finished up work early in the state capitol one day and drove back home. When she passed the courthouse, she noticed her husband's office lights were on. He was working late.

She decided to surprise him. The security guards, of course, recognized her, both as the judge's wife and as a senator, and they let her in the building.

She walked into his office behind him. He didn't know she was there. He had two computers open, and she saw what was on them. She yelled, "Oh my God, Phil! Those are children!"

"No, it's not!" He quickly shut the computers off, but Linda had already seen graphic child pornography on the screens. The children looked to be five or six years old, the same age of some of the children whose fates he decided in his role as presiding judge over DHS cases.

That was the night he broke her arm, she told Kathy. They argued. She tried to leave, but he wouldn't let her. He grabbed her arm and twisted so hard it put her on her knees.

Just then they heard keys rattling. The security guard was coming their way. Her husband let her go so she would not scream for the guard to help her.

She ran out, then filed for divorce immediately. She had endured abuse for many years for the sake of her family, but there were some things she could not live with. She said he had crossed a line and there was no going back.

Much of this information came out in the depositions with attorneys as they went through the divorce process. When Linda's attorney Kathryn Hudson asked if he had been watching pornography on his work computer, he grinned diabolically and admitted, "Yes, I have."

His attorneys immediately shut down any further questions on the subject. No one was permitted to ask questions about the child pornography Linda had seen on his computers, some of which appeared to have been filmed inside his office at the courthouse and appeared on the dark web.

David J. Sachar, Executive Director of Arkansas Judicial Discipline and Disability Commission (JDDC), filed a complaint against Judge Philip Smith on December 29, 2017, citing violations of the Arkansas Code of Judicial Conduct. The document accused him of admitting under oath, during divorce proceedings, that he "improperly used court computer equipment after regular work hours at the office." These were "extrajudicial activities that did not concern the law, the legal system, or the administration of justice."

Two days later, on December 31, 2017, Judge Smith retired from the bench.

15 - Never Forgotten

There is not a day goes by without Kathy thinking of Brooklyn, praying that somehow she can come home to her family. An email sent to Kathy's account on September 4 felt like a gut-punch when she opened it.

"Hi Kathy," the email began. "I wanted to let you know that if you or any of your family members would like to write Brooklyn letters, I will save them for her and read them to her or have them available for her to read as she gets old enough to understand the situation. I know you all love her very much." The email was signed by the woman who adopted Brooklyn as simply, "Michelle."

Kathy's heart felt as though it would rip in two. More than anything she wanted to write to her granddaughter and tell her how much she loves her and misses her every day. On the other hand, there was that "no-contact" order from Judge Zimmerman, an order requested by Michelle. If she responded, she could be held in contempt.

Tears rolled down Kathy's cheeks as she closed the email without a reply. "Please, God," she prayed. "Let Brooklyn know how much we love her. Tell her we have always wanted her."

She had to finish packing. Kathy was on her way to Washington, D.C., to join other Angel Families in sharing their stories at a couple of rallies. Linda originally planned to join them there and speak, but she came down with pneumonia and could not make it.

One rally took place on the lawn of the U.S. Capitol Building on September 7. Leaders of the group emphasized the importance of securing the border in order to reduce the kinds of crimes which took the lives of their loved ones.

White House counselor Kellyanne Conway spoke to them. "You will never be silenced, and your loved ones will never be forgotten," she told the grieving families. "Here's the truth: open borders leads to massive crime. And massive crime that is totally avoidable."[1]

~ ~ ~

Soon after the rally, Linda and Kathy were discussing the impact of illegal immigration in one of their late night phone calls. Linda proposed an idea. "Do you want to come to Little Rock and testify to the judiciary committee about this?"

"Sure. Let me make some arrangements, and I'll fly down."

"Great!"

Kathy's tone grew serious. "What do you want me to do?"

"Just tell your story." Linda reassured Kathy, "That's it. I've been talking to some other senators about this, and I want you to tell them some of the things you've been telling me."

16 - Little Rock

Less than a month later Kathy and Jeff flew in to Little Rock, Arkansas, and checked in to their hotel. Linda met them for dinner. It was the first time the two ladies met in person, but immediately they felt like they had known each other forever.

It was clear to Jeff the dinner conversation showed no signs of winding down anytime soon, so he graciously took his leave. "I'm going up to the room."

Kathy laughed. Her husband was not upset. He was simply smart enough to recognize this was to be a long night of girl talk, and he might have a better time watching TV in their hotel room.

Linda had reserved a room for herself at the same hotel, and the two friends stayed up talking into the wee hours of the morning.

The next day Linda took the Halls out sightseeing around the area.

The Senate Interim Committee on Judiciary[1] met the next morning, Monday, October 1, 2018, at 10:00 a.m. at the State House. When Kathy arrived, she was quite surprised to see Linda take her seat at the head of the room with a sign in front of her that said, "Chair." During all of their conversations, Linda had never mentioned to Kathy she was vice-chair of the judiciary committee.

Kathy knew the committee would talk about court cases involving illegal immigrants, but she was surprised, in a good way, to hear legislators and bureaucrats discussing accountability of judges, especially those involved with civil cases. It was not long before Linda narrowed the focus to specifically address judges hearing DHS cases.

The Director of the Judicial Discipline and Disability Commission (JDDC) discussed judicial policies and rules as well as oversight of judges. People who disagree with decisions of a court can appeal their cases. Senator Linda Collins-Smith asked about recourses for families who cannot afford to appeal. "We heard testimony a couple years ago about sixty-plus percent of those cases that appealed—that's just the ones that know they *can* appeal—that they're overturned."

She explained that legislators in the Judiciary Panel under Senator Alan Clark met with the AOC (Administrative Office of the Courts), the Supreme Court, and others in eighteen months of meetings. "A lot was learned in those meetings," she said, from people who testified to the panel they felt they had been wronged by DHS and the juvenile court system. Much information that was "concerning" came to light during the meetings, after which Arkansas "had several directors of departments exit the system. They were no longer employees of the state."

Legislators sought direction from the JDDC as to how to handle concerns from constituents who come to them with concerns their case was not being handled correctly. Not all of the district courts have written transcripts of the cases, the director said, which made it difficult to find out exactly what is happening in a specific courtroom when the JDDC received complaints on a judge. It made accountability harder.

Senator Collins-Smith said, "I think people know I have all respect for judges that do their job. Your day in court—if you've never been in front of a judge—it's a scary thing, because they rule. And if that judge is not attentive, or if that judge is not doing their job, it's very concerning."

She pressed the question of how the public can learn about judges with complaints against them. It is difficult for anyone, including the JDDC and legislators, to find out when a particular judge has similar complaints which are recurring, but she said the public has a right to know.

In situations where legislators tried to get case files from courts and DHS, they have often been stonewalled. She told the committee she ran into a brick wall working with a family trying to obtain records from the department. She did not mention any names, but Kathy knew Linda was referring specifically to her case. She said there was something wrong when even the head of the judiciary committee could not get their hands on a particular case file.

It took months of requests before DHS sent Senator Collins-Smith the case files about Hailey and Brooklyn. When they finally arrived, she realized the files were incomplete. What's more, every page they sent was written in the same handwriting. The ink was the same on all the documents—same color ink and same width of pen on every single page. Linda told Kathy the documents looked like they had all been freshly filled out, all by the same person. There was simply no way these were the original documents over the year and a half of the case.

Even so, Linda did not address these discrepancies during the course of the judicial hearing; she simply wanted to bring attention to the fact that DHS was trying to hide information from the very people entrusted to hold the department accountable. The court told the senator the recordings of the court hearings regarding Brooklyn must have been misplaced because they had not been able to locate them.

Kathy did not realize at the time that Senator Clark had run into similar problems in 2015-16 when trying to get DHS records on Hal Stanley's case; however, the committee knew about it. Senator Clark wrote in October 2016 about his efforts to obtain information on the Stanley case: "Most do not know that I had to hold the DCFS [Department of Children and Family Services] budget to get that information and the whole Arkansas legislature had to back me to force them to comply. They are clearly more secretive than they have to be. They are clearly more secretive than the law allows."[2]

The problems that existed then had still not been resolved, and Senator Collins-Smith wanted to know how legislators could do their job of serving constituents when facing such lack of transparency within DHS and the judiciary.

The Senator had heard from quite a number of her constituents that they were not getting a fair hearing in court, and their families were being destroyed. If a judge allows children to be taken wrongfully or adopted out wrongfully, she stressed, "it's just unacceptable. You just can't fix that problem." Parents go before judges who literally have the right to decide if they will ever see their own child again, and they are understandably scared. "They just want a fair hearing. They want to know it's fair."

Kathy's ears perked up when she heard Senator Alan Clark ask about relative placement of children taken by DHS. The law states children are to go to relatives as the first choice, but it does not always happen. Kathy knew this firsthand. While foster care agencies beg for foster parents for all of the children they have in their custody, they leave out the part where the majority of those children have family members who are ready, willing, and able to step in and care for their own relatives.

A dirty little secret of the industry is that there is more federal money available to states when children are removed from their homes, placed with strangers, and adopted out to strangers. One of many federal funding streams states can access comes through the Adoption and Safe Families Act of 1997 (ASFA).[3] States do not receive any ASFA dollars if children are reunited with their families, or if they are placed with relatives. These funds only become available when states adopt foster children out to strangers, providing a perverse incentive for Child Welfare agencies to bypass relative placement in favor of people the children do not know.

ASFA provides additional bonuses for adopting out more children than in the previous year, and for adoption of special needs children, which can mean something as simple as more than two children in the same family or older children as well as those with disabilities.

Senator Clark wanted to know what could be done about judges adopting children out to strangers when there were relatives they could live with who were qualified. He had found that some judges do a great job, while others do not.

He told the committee about a military man whose niece was taken by DHS while he was stationed out of state. The very next day, he said, the man and his wife started working to get the baby placed with them. They put in for a transfer and moved back to driving distance so one of them could move into Arkansas. Though the soldier had a perfect record, the judge denied them their niece based on them living out of state. She was adopted out to strangers.

At the Termination of Parental Rights (TPR) hearing, the judge coldly told them, "Decisions have consequences." He meant, Senator Clark explained, "that their service in the military had consequences to them not being able to adopt."

He asked the JDDC director "Is that actionable? Or do we have to sit back and say we'll have to allow judges to be able to make decisions, so we have to live with garbage like that?"

"Depends on what you mean by 'actionable.'" Obviously, the director explained, laws cannot be written so narrowly that judges have no discretion. However, if there is clear bias, such as appeared to be the case here, there could be sanctions placed on the judge. He then explained what essentially amounts to a slap on the wrist with no consequences. The committee could issue a corrective action, whereby the judge could say, "I'm sorry. I won't do that in the future." However, it would not change the outcome for the family whose child was stripped away from them.

Later in the hearing, they discussed the fact that it was currently up to individual judges to decide if they will recuse themselves if there is a conflict of interests, further indicating the need for transparency.

Another issue Senator Collins-Smith brought up was the fact that she heard over and over from the public that their lawyers would not file this motion or that document needed in their case. When the lawyers were questioned, their explanation was they had to work in that courtroom and they were afraid of the judge, "for fear of eating in the future"—yet another situation which makes it difficult for families to find true justice in the courts.

They wrapped up the segment of the hearing acknowledging there was much work still to be done, then moved into discussion of illegal immigration.

For this part, Senator Collins-Smith brought in several prosecutors, mayors, and state police, as well as Kathy Hall. The point of this segment was to answer the questions, "Are we consistent in arrests in the state of Arkansas?" and "Are we consistent in the way people are punished if they are illegal aliens?"

According to an interview she did with *New Right Network*,[4] the senator said she learned that the state troopers handled things consistently throughout the state. However, at the city and county levels, they were not consistent; neither were the prosecutors.

The judiciary committee discussed the detention of illegals who were arrested for other crimes. The U.S. Immigration and Customs Enforcement (ICE) and the prosecuting attorney's office are required to be notified if an illegal immigrant is arrested for a serious crime. Bob McMahon from the Office of Prosecutor Coordinator explained to the committee the process of considering such individuals a flight risk, noting that judges and prosecutors may take flight risks under advisement if they become aware of it.

Kathy Hall then told the committee the story of Sergio Rodriguez, without calling him by name, and his hit-and-run of her daughter and David. She described how bystanders heard David's screams for help. Sergio had to have walked right past him after parking his truck, yet he ignored his cries and fled the scene. When he turned himself in two days later, he was able to quickly bond out—in less than two hours.

Beer bottles were found at the crime scene, but because he hid out for two days, police did not test him for alcohol or drugs. Kathy was told the tests would not show anything at that point. Kathy said, "We don't know that the man was drunk."

This led to a conversation with a police chief who agreed this is a problem with hit-and-run crimes. When a perpetrator leaves the scene, proof of intoxication is often unavailable by the time he is caught or turns himself in. Had he remained at the scene and been proven intoxicated, the penalty for his crimes likely would have been much stronger. The chief called for legislators to enact stiffer penalties for hit-and-runs, penalties severe enough to encourage perpetrators to stay on scene.

He also stated he was familiar with Kathy's case. He noted the perpetrator of the crimes hired an attorney who was an ex-prosecutor who knew the ropes. That is how he was able to bond out so quickly after turning himself in.

It became clear through the meeting there is inconsistency within the state of how serious crimes committed by illegals are handled.

The meeting adjourned at 12:20 p.m. It was a long meeting, but Kathy was thankful to have been there. She hoped her daughter's story helped open some eyes within the judiciary committee to some of the problems plaguing families in Arkansas (and other states) dealing with CPS as well as illegal immigration.

Linda still had a full afternoon of legislative work ahead of her, so they made plans to meet that night for dinner. Kathy went back to her hotel room for some much-needed rest.

That night at dinner, they again talked for hours.

"You don't know how hard I have been working on this legislation." Linda told Kathy about bills they had worked on to rein in the almost-omnipotent power of Child Protective Services. She explained that a couple of other legislators were more "the face" of the legislation, but she worked very hard behind the scenes.

Linda leaned across the table. "I found out that DHS has a second set of books."

"They what?" Kathy put down her fork.

In her digging around, Linda had found that the department kept a second set of books, with major financial discrepancies between the two. Many millions of dollars were missing, and she wanted to know where the money went.

At one time, legislators believed that twenty-eight million dollars were missing. By the time she was no longer in office, she discovered it was closer to the fifty to sixty million dollar range.[5]

Kathy and Jeff flew back to Colorado the next morning.

As Kathy stared out the window at the clouds, she reflected on the past few days. She had heard Linda's passion for justice in their many phone conversations, but it was something else entirely to see the dauntless fire in her eyes in person. Clearly Linda was not one to sit back quietly when she believed she could do something about it.

When they first spoke on the phone, Kathy had given up hope than any politician would help her. Now, she was on her way home after watching Linda in action. She was truly a force to be reckoned with. Kathy was thankful their paths had crossed. But it was more than that. Their hearts connected. Kathy felt like they'd known each other forever. There was no doubt she and Linda were friends for life.

From that point forward, they talked just about every day—often four or five times a day.

Both Kathy and Linda regularly spoke with media and did interviews. Most of the interviews centered on illegal immigration because that was what the media was interested in.

Behind the scenes, however, Linda never stopped digging to try to find out exactly what was going on with DHS. The more she dug, the more she realized the rabbit hole went deeper than she ever could have imagined, and it circled back to her own back yard.

17 - Family Forward Project

Linda's divorce decree came through on October 12. She was relieved to be free of the marriage, but the judge's decision about the division of marital property left her in a difficult position. In cases where there is marital property involved, it is common for judges to order the properties sold and the parties split the net profits. That did not happen.

Instead, Judge Ellen Brantley awarded the properties which had equity and no debt to her former colleague, retired Judge Phil Smith, leaving the properties with debt remaining on them to Linda. Many of these, including her Pocahontas home, were undergoing renovations.

The judge ordered Linda to remove Phil's name from the properties within sixty days—an impossible task since Linda's term, and thus her income, as a Senator would end at the end of the year. That, combined with insufficient equity in the properties left to her, made her unable to refinance the loans and allow Phil's name to be removed.

She filed a notice to appeal the court's decision a month after the decree was filed.[1] Two months after the divorce, Phil remarried.

Family Forward Project

~ ~ ~

"There is a rally coming up in Little Rock about DCS." Linda told Kathy she should check it out.

The December 10 rally was sponsored by the Family Forward Foundation, a national non-profit organization founded by attorney and family rights advocate Connie Reguli of Tennessee. The group's motto is "Making family integrity and child safety work together in our homes and our nation."

As an attorney for more than twenty years, Connie saw repeated abuse of families by the child protective system. She created a Facebook group called Family Forward Project in 2015 to reach out to support and encourage families across the United States who are fighting Child Protective Services for their children. The grassroots group had almost nineteen thousand members as of late 2023. There are Family Forward groups on Facebook for each of the fifty states.

Senator Alan Clark was a featured speaker as well as Joe Churchwell, Arkansas attorney for Hal Stanley, whose homeschooled children were unjustly taken from their home by DHS.

Neither Linda nor Kathy were able to attend in person. Linda posted the livestream of the event[2] on her Facebook page, and she watched it online, interacting with the event through real-time comments on the feed.

Connie Reguli started off the rally by encouraging attendees—most of whom were victims of DHS—to send postcards to their federal legislators to "Ban ASFA." The Adoption and Safe Families Act of 1997 (ASFA) is one of the major federal funding streams which enables states to take children from their families and adopt them out to strangers, to the tune of billions of dollars each year. One or two such postcards can easily be overlooked, but if lawmakers are getting a thousand of these, they are harder to ignore.

She urged the parents to get their stories out to the public. "People need to see your stories."

"Here's what is happening—our society is normalizing a social engineering project that takes children from their birth parents and the government decides who would be a better parent." She said she has seen children taken out of homes because the parents reached out for help. They can be taken with or without evidence, and this is not the American way.

Many of the issues brought up that day were the same ones the AK Judiciary Committee discussed earlier. Connie and Joe Churchwell discussed the failure of Child Protective Services to place children with relatives, unrealistic case plans, and the fact that there is no real accountability for the department. There is often no remedy for parents who were treated unjustly and no penalty for those within the system who do wrong. Social workers, such as some in the Hal Stanley case, fabricate evidence and even plant evidence without consequence.

They said the government agencies involved often use the law to protect itself, not the people they serve. Money and contracts are funneled through non-profits and kickbacks to legislators. Case workers, attorneys, and judges within the system who do wrong are frequently given a pass by the justice system.

Senator Alan Clark took the floor and pointed out that the Arkansas legislature passed four good laws regarding DHS that year, which took several legislators working together. The governor signed them into law.

He talked about the problem of "state abuse"—abuse of children and families by the state. This includes family members being passed over or ignored for placement of the children.

Linda agreed. She posted a comment on the livestream. "So true. The DHS has free reign to do what they want. My heart breaks. No accountability with judges who do wrong or DHS agents who do wrong. Not mistakes but intentionally wrong."

Legislators often do not believe this can happen unless they see it for themselves. Senator Clark acknowledged the skepticism in the audience about there being good case workers. "I know some of you don't think so, but we have a lot of wonderful people that work within the system. But we have some bullies. And because it's not transparent, they get away with some things."

Linda posted, "Legislators have to take time to listen. Once they do they won't be able to move on to other things because it can be their children or grandchildren this happens to."

"And we'll move these kids around like playing cards," Senator Clark continued, "but we *know*—when we've had the experts come testify, we know it's traumatic to take the kids out of their homes the first time. But we know it's traumatic every time we move them, and the more we do that, the more long-term damage that there is."

He addressed the serious problem of transparency. "Part of the reason that we have the problem we have is because it's dark, because it's not transparent the way the rest of our system is transparent, and doesn't protect children and families. It protects wrongdoers."

"It protects wrongdoers!!" Linda agreed.

"It protects the judges doing the wrong thing," he continued. "It protects the case worker and investigator and DCFS attorneys doing the wrong thing. So we've got to have more transparency."

Many things that get reported to CPS are not actually abuse. The Arkansas Senate passed a parents' rights bill stating that DHS would not investigate certain things reported to them like letting children walk to the park and back or walk home from school. "If that gets turned in, we just don't investigate it." However, the House failed to pass the bill. Idaho later became the first state to pass such a bill. Idaho called it the "Free-Range Parenting Bill."

The Senator stated his intention to re-file the bill in the next session. "What we've done is we've caused young parents to be afraid to parent."

Linda added her input, "Make sure you change the hotline reporting." Sometimes families are investigated and children removed over anonymous reports from a disgruntled neighbor, a vindictive ex, or a relative who simply disagrees with the parents' style of parenting.

"That's where do-gooders are being nosy." Senator Clark got to the heart of the real reason the public supports Child Protective Services. "These laws were not passed for that. These laws were passed for people who were burning kids, who were locking kids in closets, and starving kids, and we've got to stop those kinds of things. We've got to punish people who do those kind of things and deal with those kind of things, but we can't treat everybody else like they're guilty. We cannot act like this is Germany in World War II and this is a police state. We have to stop acting like that."

He found no disagreement with those statements in the room. Parents whose children were taken unjustly are often the first to demand punishment for people who truly abuse children. They are confused by a system which frequently turns a blind eye to real abuse and covers it up, all the while taking children from loving parents who want the best for their children.

Several families stayed behind after the speakers finished speaking to tell their stories on camera with Connie Reguli.

Photo provided by Family Forward Project.

18 - Scars and Fears

Christmas was approaching. The lights and decorations were up, and most of the presents were wrapped. Gingerbread cookies were in the oven and the house smelled yummy, but Kathy's heart was heavy.

A close friend had just confided to her that she found her husband on a dating website. When she confronted her husband, he shifted the blame onto her, accusing her of being too busy to pay attention to him. The conversation was fresh on Kathy's mind when Linda texted her about a possible interview with Alex Jones.

"Someone else mentioned trying to get him to join us." Kathy had heard the name but did not know who he was. "Who is he?"

Linda was not really familiar with the *Infowars* host either. "That is my question."

"Lol ok. I'll find out. Can I ask you a personal question? How long did it take you once you decided to leave your husband to actually leave?"

Linda took a few minutes to answer her text. "Too many years. I stayed way too long, and it got dangerous."

Kathy recalled some of their previous conversations. Her heart went out to Linda. "Yeah, I bet. Thanks for that."

She told Linda what was going on with her friend. What made it worse was that it was right at Christmas time. "I think a lot of men actually enjoy seeing women hurt."

"Phil did and especially when it cut deep emotionally or physically like a sick high or sex high. He won every time he got there."

"You are very strong and brave to have stayed." Kathy knew Linda's faith was very important to her, and that was at least part of the reason she stayed with him so long.

Linda opened up more about her marriage. She texted, "Also beat me down emotionally. Keeping my family together meant so much. Sad. I should not have walked down that aisle."

The oven timer dinged, and Kathy took the cookies out of the oven. After the next batch went in, she read the next text.

"Yes ma'am. Never wait so long. I am for giving every ounce of effort even when my husband doesn't. It broke me down personally. Outward, I am always the same — serious. Business was Momma etc Etc. But at home he was a nightmare."

"I am so sorry."

"Phil was mean and worse at times. He was abusive and we did not live together for a few years and people didn't know it."

Kathy recalled previous conversations where Linda told her that her colleagues and co-workers suspected she was being abused, but she hid it, for the sake of her family. Sunglasses covered up a black eye; long sleeves covered bruises, and so on. She never talked about the abuse to any of her family until the divorce. Because she hid it so long, when she finally started talking about it, some of the people she loved were skeptical.

Kathy picked up the phone and called Linda. "Did he ever hit the kids?"

"Oh, no." Linda explained that her ex-husband was a master at hiding what he did to her. He never hit the kids, and he never hit her in front of them either. It was all behind closed doors. She always tried not to scream out because she didn't want her kids to know. She wanted desperately for her children to have a good family and structure in their life, so she tried hard to keep her family together. Sometimes they would hear her yell and things banging. "That wasn't me throwing things at him; that was him throwing ME."

The weight of Linda's words hung in the air. Kathy didn't know what to say, except, "I am so glad you got out."

"Me, too."

~ ~ ~

New Year 2019 meant Linda's time in the Arkansas Senate was at an end. She left behind her title as a legislator as well as the "-Smith" from her last name. She was divorced, but she carried the scars with her into the new year.

While Kathy planned another trip to DC with the Angel Families in January, Linda—Collins now—went into surgery to have pins removed from her arm. Even though her arm was broken a couple years before, the pins still caused her a great deal of pain. Besides the physical pain, the memory of the circumstances surrounding the injury never left her.

Linda sent a text to Kathy, "Call tonight."

When Kathy did not respond, Linda texted the next morning, "I didn't hear from you. Want to talk in a little while or tonight?"

Kathy explained she meant to call her but time got away from her. "Before I knew it last night, it was 11:30."

"Kathy, I have to talk. Are you OK? Please call ASAP."

Linda sounded urgent. She had reason to. Her ex-husband tried to break into her home in Pocahontas, and it was not the first time. She put objects in the windows to keep him from getting in, but it didn't stop him. This time she found footprints outside in the dirt by one of the windows.

"Have you told the police?"

"Yes. They came out but they refuse to file a report."

"Why?"

"They say they can't prove it was him."

"Do they think the footprints by the window got there by themselves?" Kathy's voice dripped with sarcasm.

Linda's voice carried frustration alongside fear. "I've called 911 several times about him trying to break in." All in all, she called 911 on eight different occasions from her cell phone in her house about Phil trying to break in. "It's just like when we were married. I call 911 to report domestic violence. They send somebody out, but they ignore me. They act like I am crazy and just blow it all off—I guess because of who he is. And they don't file reports."

"Why don't you put security cameras up?" Kathy suggested. "Then they can't deny it's going on because you have it on camera."

"That's actually a great idea."

Soon after, Linda had security cameras installed all around the house.

19 - She Had it All Along

Kathy carried a 10 x 13 photo of Hailey to a press conference on Capitol Hill, held by Women for Trump on January 15, 2019.[1]

She joined several other Angel Families holding pictures of their loved ones who were lost to crimes committed by people in the country illegally. Among the speakers at the event were Representative Louie Gohmert of Texas and former ICE Director Tom Homan.

Partisan politics were in play as President Trump and many Republicans were in a political stand-off with Democrat Representatives over funding of a wall at the U.S./Mexico border and a partial government shutdown.

After the press conference, the group made their way to the legislative buildings to talk with their Congressmen about the importance of securing the border.

House Speaker Nancy Pelosi refused to see them. Citizen vloggers with Women for America First posted video[2] of the scene at Pelosi's office on Facebook. Sabine Durden, the mother of a son killed by an illegal in 2012, said all they wanted was for Congress-woman Pelosi to "come see all of us in one room. No press, just us, just for two minutes."

They wanted the legislator to SEE them, to see their pain, and to see the real-life consequences of lax border security. Some of the parents felt they had been slapped in the face or sucker-punched when she refused to see them. Kathy asked where Nancy Pelosi's compassion was.

Since they could not tell Pelosi in person about their stories, several of the families briefly shared their stories with people who videotaped them. Media outlets including *Breitbart*[3] and *FOX News'* Sean Hannity[4] picked up on the story.

The group talked to other legislators as they walked the halls of Congress. When they reached the office of Senate Minority Leader Chuck Schumer, they were again rebuffed.[5] Like Pelosi, he did not appear to want to hear from the families of victims killed as a result of DC policies.

After a week of meetings with various legislators and media, Kathy returned home to Colorado. While Linda was home in Arkansas recuperating from her surgery, she developed pneumonia and went back to the hospital.

Kathy turned around and flew out to San Diego with the founder of Angel Families, Mary Ann Mendoza, for a rally.

She had only been home a week or so from California when she got a call from Angel Families. President Trump was expected to call a national emergency at the border, and the presence of the Angel Families was requested.

There was no hesitation as Kathy quickly agreed to go back to Washington, D.C. She called Linda to tell her the news.

"I would love to go with you!" Thankfully, Linda was recovered from being sick and was ready to get back in action. "I can just be there as your friend for support."

"That would be awesome, but it's pretty pricey. We stay at the Trump Tower, but I have my own room. You're more than welcome to share it with me."

"Great! I can do that!"

"Would you like to speak? I know there will be events that week where you can speak. I can get that arranged."

"No. I would be going as support for you, Kathy. Not to be political."

She Had it All Along

"Let's do it!"

A few days later, on February 11, Kathy posted a photo of the lobby of the Trump Hotel and commented, "Packing for another trip to Washington DC tomorrow. Angel families are on the go once again. Let's pray that it makes a difference. Best part is the hotel!"

The two friends arrived in DC on their respective flights the next day. After checking into their room, they met with some of the Angel Families for dinner to discuss plans for the next few days—a whirlwind of meetings with legislators, rallies, and other events. The dinnertime discussion was filled with stories from the parents, and they updated each other with reports of the status of upcoming legislature in their respective states.

When they got back to their room, Linda sank into a chair and let out a big sigh. Kathy sensed she had something weighing heavily on her mind. She was not wrong.

"You're not going to believe what I found."

"What did you find?"

"It's probably not even safe for me to tell you." Linda glanced around the room cautiously, like she was afraid the walls had ears. "Remember what I told you about what I saw on Phil's computers in his office?"

"The day he broke your arm? Yeah. Awful."

"I have it."

She wasn't making sense to Kathy. "You have it? You have what? What do you have?"

"The computer. One of Phil's computers. I've had it all along, but I didn't know it."

"THE computer, the one with the child porn on it? What?! How?"

Linda explained she had recently been going through some of the boxes at her house looking for something else. There it was—her ex-husband's computer. Somehow, when she and Phil split up their things during the divorce, the box with his computer ended up with her stuff that went with her when she moved. It was one of the two computers she had seen him looking at when she surprised him in his office. It had been in her house all along, but she didn't realize it until recently when she found it buried in a box in a pile of boxes.

She was still stunned at what she saw. Linda was able to figure out her ex's password to see some of what was on it, but there was more on there that she could not access yet.

What she was able to see was horrific. There were names, places, and things she never wanted to see, and they connected many of the pieces she had been trying to put together for a long time.

Linda shuddered to think what could possibly be in the parts of the computer she could not access.

She was still early in the process of finding out what was stored on the computer, but what she knew already and told Kathy about that night was staggering. She and Kathy had been hearing whispers from parents all over the county of their children being used for child sex trafficking. Now, it looked like these whispers were being confirmed by the things Linda saw on her ex-husband's computer.

At this point, Linda was trying to process what she had found, and she had to figure out what to do with the information. It was hard to know who to trust. Children were being violated and hurt, and she desperately wanted to help them.

"Are you going to the police about this?" Kathy asked.

Linda threw up her hands in frustration. "How? Which ones? There is no point in going to the police at home. They are the ones who refused to even do a police report all the times I called when Phil tried to break in. Would they cover for him? Will the information disappear? Or worse?"

"Good questions," Kathy admitted wryly.

They talked into the wee hours of the morning. Kathy could not say who fell asleep first, but eventually the conversation wound down.

20 - Angel Families

The next day, February 13, was a busy day, starting with a 10:00 a.m. rally outside the Capitol building.[1] The Angel Families were the main event for the rally by a coalition of groups including America First Policies, Women for Trump, Women for America First, and Advocates for Victims of Illegal Alien Crime.

Several Republican lawmakers spoke at the event.

Representative Steve Scalise addressed the group: "Our hearts and our prayers are with the families of everybody who's lost a loved one because someone who was here illegally took their life. It shouldn't happen. It shouldn't happen in America, and thank God we have Donald Trump who not only campaigned and said he would build the wall, but has fought to secure our border to keep America safe."[2]

Congress was currently in the middle of heated debates over funding and building over 500 additional miles of a border wall. After Rep. Scalise, several other legislators, and a sheriff spoke of the importance of making that happen, the Angel Families spoke, sharing their heartbreaking stories one after another.

While those with ears to hear listened to grieving parents and family members pour out their hearts, tourists and sightseers were captured on video wandering around and behind the Angel Families, utterly oblivious to their pain, not realizing any one of them could be one tragedy away from joining the group nobody wants to be a part of.

When it was Kathy's turn to speak, she shared that her daughter's killer would be up for parole after just two years in prison—a man who was allowed to marry a U.S. citizen right before being sentenced.

She read a social media post written by Hailey which ended, "Remember my name, because I am Hailey Cyell King, and one day I am going to do very big things."

Kathy willed herself to hold her voice firm and strong. "She never got a chance to do those things."

This is bigger than just the injustice that happened to her family, she explained, and she wanted people to know that good legislators sometimes vote against good-sounding bills because the bills are too weak to be effective or contain bad things in them. She thanked Senator Tom Cotton of Arkansas for being one of those who stood strong in such cases.

"Also, our state senator Linda Collins-Smith—she has been there for me and for a lot of us, and still to this day has done everything that she can to be there for us. She is here with me to be by my side." Kathy turned to Linda with a grateful smile, "and I want to thank you."

She asked if Linda wanted to come speak, but she declined. Linda was there to support Kathy. This was about her and the other Angel Families being heard. Parents continued to share their stories—a lifetime of memories, love, and pain, condensed to brief two or three-minute speeches for the cameras and legislators.

When it was Angel Mom Melanie Kortlang's turn, she shared the story of her daughter Amy, age twenty-two, who was killed by an illegal. It was the drunk driver's fifth DUI. He had been deported three times, but he kept coming back.

She wore her child's ashes in a tiny urn necklace around her neck as she gave an impassioned speech, indicating the photos of loved ones being held up by Angel Families. "Look at all these beautiful faces, lives cut way too soon, way too short.

And it's time to make these fools listen to us [indicating the legislators in the Capitol building]. Enough is enough! We need to build the damn wall! We need security on our borders. And LISTEN to us!"

Her grief was palpable as she read a letter to her daughter. "Dear Amy, I miss you so much," she began. "... I will never let you be forgotten. I made a promise to her as she lay in that coffin that her death will not be in vain...." She left the podium with tears streaming down her face.

Other family members spoke out. They came from all over America—from border states and interior states, from red states and blue states. One had a story dating back decades; another shared a story less than two months old. The victims were children, teens, mothers, and fathers, from all walks of life—from students to an FBI agent. Their killers ranged in age and countries of origin, some with long criminal histories, all in the United States illegally.

Wendy Corcoran, Angel Mom, and Avery Corcoran, Angel Sister, lost their son/brother Pierce Kennedy Corcoran, age twenty-two, on December 29, 2018, to a man in the U.S. illegally for fourteen years after his work visa expired. The man plowed his vehicle into oncoming traffic causing a chain-reaction wreck. He had no driver's license and no insurance. Yet "we [taxpayers] provide his legal counsel."

Sabine Durden, Angel Mom, buried her thirty-year-old son Dominic, a beloved volunteer firefighter. His killer had a long arrest record, including two prior DUIs, and was driving without a license when he ended Dominic's life on July 12, 2012. Sabine asked, "Why would some of our politicians fight harder for illegals than Americans? Many questions; no answers."

Susan Stevens, Angel Mom, explained how the influx of illegal drugs over the border, including opioids and fentanyl, has led to hundreds of deaths a day in the U.S. Her "golden child" daughter Toria became addicted to opioids after a violent rape left her with severe PTSD. At age twenty-two, she lost her battle with addiction on January 22, 2018. With the vast majority of these drugs coming into the country illegal over the southern border, Susan blames lax border policies for her daughter's death.

Kathy Woods, Angel Mom, and Shelly Woods, Angel Sister, held up a photo showing seventeen-year-old Steve Wood on one side, flashing a smile for a school picture. The other side showed an x-ray of Steve's skull, pierced through with a sharpened paint-roller rod. Steve was hanging out with friends at the beach when they were attacked by a gang of nine illegal aliens. Three of the nine got away scot-free because they were not read their Miranda rights. Only two of the remaining six are still in prison.

Kiyan Michael said her son Brandon Michael was killed by a man who had already been deported twice. Brandon was on his lunch break in Virginia to cash his paycheck on August 15. 2007. After the killer hit Brandon's car and flipped it, he got out of his car and watched as Brandon took his last breath. He only served a two year sentence.

Lori and Gene Vargus of San Antonio, Texas, told the story of their twenty-year-old son Jared, brutally murdered and his body set on fire seven months earlier, on June 18, 2018. The killer had a history of being in and out of police custody and had been given a voluntary deportation order just two weeks before murdering Jared.

Dan Ferguson, Angel Dad of Amanda Ferguson Weyant, twenty-eight-year-old elementary schoolteacher, said the man who killed his daughter had a criminal history and had already been deported before. He came back into the U.S. and was arrested, jailed, and released on aggravated assault charges. On Thanksgiving morning 2018, the man got drunk and blew through two red lights before killing Amanda in a crosswalk. Dan told *KFOX14 News*, "He didn't even attempt to stop to render aid."[3]

Michelle Root's daughter Sarah, age twenty-one, was killed in Omaha, Nebraska. She had graduated that night from Bellevue University with a 4.0 GPA and was on her way home. She was rear-ended at a stoplight by a drunk illegal going over 70 mph in a 35-mph zone. He had a prior failure to appear warrant for child endangerment after driving the wrong way down a one-way street. After killing Sarah, he spent five days in jail before posting bond and hasn't been seen since.[4]

Marla Wolff lost her husband, thirty-six-year-old FBI special agent Carlos Wolff, on December 18, 2017. Following a single-vehicle car accident, Carlos was joined by Deputy Chief Fire Marshal Sander Cohen on the shoulder of the highway when Roberto Garza Palacios ran into them, killing both Carlos and Sander. Palacios already had two DUIs on his record, as well as two counts of endangerment, possession of cocaine, and more by the time of his Christmas season crash. He was released on fifteen thousand dollars bail and not deported.

Vickie Lyon's daughter Nikki of Florida was killed instantly in 2001 by an illegal who was driving on the wrong side of the road. He had already run five cars off the road before plowing into Nikki's vehicle, leaving her dead and her two small children needing to be airlifted to the hospital. After eighteen years, the killer has yet to serve a single day in jail.

Boni Driskell, Angel Mom of fifteen-year-old Lacy Marie Ferguson, held up a photo of her daughter and read a letter she wrote to Lacy, who was killed by a drunk driver in the country illegally. She held her daughter's hand as she slipped away from this life.

Marie Vega's son, Javier Jr., was a former Marine Corp Corporal and a border patrol agent. He was murdered in front of his parents and his family while on a fishing trip. The two men who shot him during the attempted robbery had been deported a combined six times prior to their attack on the Vegas and were believed to have Cartel connections.[5]

Angie Vargas lost her thirteen-year-old son Reuben to a gang member who was in their town for the Christmas holidays. His killer fled back to Mexico where he was apprehended. He was sentenced in Mexico to twenty years. The last time Angie held Reuben in her arms, she told him how much she loved him and that if anything ever happened to him, she would die. "But I was wrong," she said. "I didn't die." Her loss made her stronger and she works every day to keep her promise to him on the day he died to help his friends and others like him.

Don Rosenberg's son Drew was a law student in San Francisco. He was killed in November 2010 by an illegal trying to make a last-second left-hand turn. The man tried to back up and flee, running over him a second time. He ran over him a third time and was stopped by a "brave man" who stood in front of the car. It took five men to lift the car off Drew's battered body. Don wonders what it will take for people to listen.

Dennis Bixby, Angel Dad of Amanda Kate Bixby, age nineteen, told how his daughter was killed by an illegal who eluded a police sobriety check point. He turned down a back road, critically injuring three people and killing Amanda. He spent a total of eight hours in jail, was fined $170, then turned loose into the community. Dennis said he has seen the huge walls around Speaker of the House Nancy Pelosi's house, and they work. "This is our country, and I want it back."

Agnes Gibboney is a legal immigrant from Hungary. Her son, Ronald de Silva, age twenty-nine, was killed on April 27, 2002. He was ambushed, shot, and killed in his driveway by an illegal alien who was also a gang member who had been deported at least once. In response to politicians who spouted soundbites to the media about the border crisis being a "manufactured crisis," she held up a photo of her son's gravestone and said bitterly, "This is not manufactured."

Cynthia Scalf lost her firstborn child, thirty-seven-year-old Shirra Branum, on March 16, 2017, in a head-on collision with a drunk illegal on probation for his third DUI. At the time of Shirra's death, the killer was scheduled for a bond for deportation hearing. Shirra left behind daughters and a son.

Laura Wilkerson, Angel Mom, told the story of her son Joshua who died on November 16, 2010. He was mercilessly, violently beaten, tortured, strangled, and set on fire by an illegal alien classmate who asked Joshua for a ride home from school. Instead of her son coming home, she got an autopsy report. His killer came to America at age ten with parents on a six-month work Visa. The parents overstayed, and their son became a vicious killer. Laura was grateful to Joshua for leaving behind Scriptures that comfort her now, but she is tired of illegals getting leniency in our court system.

Judy Zieto of Louisiana wrapped up the testimonies by telling the story of her blue-eyed son Blake Michael Zieto, age twenty, who was killed in a hit-and-run on November 18, 2006. The killer had already committed two crimes, but was not deported. Six months after his second criminal offense, he ran over Blake and his motorcycle. He fled the scene and left Blake under his burning truck. Men lifted the flaming truck off of Blake and he was flown by helicopter to the hospital. He died in the helicopter. Jesus Maltose Chican has never been captured and is still wanted for vehicular homicide. Blake always wanted to be a firefighter and save lives. Judy said, "We protected you your whole life, but we couldn't protect you or save you that day." She promised her son she would seek justice for his senseless death.

These stories are but a tiny portion of similar stories happening all over America. Representative Mo Brooks of Huntsville, Alabama, told Democrat lawmakers they are guilty of "aiding and abetting" the homicides of close to two thousand Americans in 2018 by illegal aliens because of their open borders policies and porous southern border.[6]

The group spent the rest of the day walking up and down the halls of the Congressional office buildings. When they passed the old-time phone booths on the first floor of the Longworth Office Building, Linda wanted to stop for photos. The pay phones have long since been gone, but she smiled for the camera as she pretended to talk on her red cell phone which matched her bright red coat.

There were scheduled meetings and hoped-for meetings with legislators and media. Just as she did in January, Speaker of the House Nancy Pelosi refused to see the Angel Families for a second time.

Linda later told the *New Right Network* what she thought about the Speaker of the House's response. "They should be respectful of the people that have them in office. It's very offensive to go to Nancy Pelosi's office and see a partial wall that protects her from the people. They need to remember, these people are dying. They are hurt. Think of the money we can have for security if we didn't have to spend it all on illegals."[7]

Their meeting with Senator Tom Cotton went much better. Immigration and the border were important issues to him. They also met with other legislators who seemed interested in talking with them.

Senator Tom Cotton tweeted a photo and comment about their meeting. "Today I met with Kathy Hall, an Angel Mom whose daughter was killed in a hit-and-run by an individually unlawfully present in Arkansas. These cases are tragic and they are all unnecessary. This is another reminder of why we need to enforce our immigration."

All in all, though it was a long day, they felt it was a good day. That evening Kathy and Linda went back to their room to freshen up for dinner.

21 - Adventures in DC

Kathy and Linda met some of the Angel Families group in the hotel restaurant. After ordering something to eat, several of the ladies peppered Linda with questions on how to talk effectively to legislators. Kathy smiled; Linda was in her element, listening to the stories and giving advice on how to get the ear of their legislators and work to get bills changed or passed.

While they waited for their food, Kathy slipped outside with another Angel Mom for a cigarette.

There were other patrons and guests outside as well, but they paid no attention as they were quickly deep in conversation about their common experiences.

"Did I hear Arkansas? Are you from Arkansas?" An extremely well-dressed man in a suit and tie interrupted them.

"Well," replied Kathy. "I was living in Arkansas."

"Let's go for a ride," the man said, smiling as he gestured towards a limo.

"Um, I'm not getting in any car with you and going anywhere." Kathy was certainly not looking for any crazy adventure in the capitol city. *Was the man off his rocker?*

"You're safe! Go get your friends, whoever you want. Come on, let's go for a ride. Let me show you the town."

Kathy laughed. "I'll tell you what. I'll go talk to one of my friends about it."

As she walked a few feet away over to the door of the Trump Hotel, the doorman said, "Excuse me, Mrs. Hall, but you are safe if you go with him."

"Ohhhh-kay," she said hesitantly. "I don't know who that man is."

"That is someone you WANT to go take a ride with," the doorman assured her confidently. "There is no one in this hotel right now that you would be safer with."

Seriously? I can't believe this! "OK, are you sure?"

"Yes, ma'am," he replied. "You should take the senator with you."

"Hmmm. Well, I'm going to get her right now and talk to her." Kathy could not explain it logically, but she believed the doorman. Her brain said this was crazy, but, somehow, she felt safe.

The other Angel Mom with Kathy quietly listened to the whole conversation. She was up for the adventure and dashed upstairs to get her daughter who was also a part of the Angel Families group.

Kathy went inside to the table, and beckoned, "Linda? Hey, come outside with me a minute."

Linda's food had just arrived at that moment. She took a bite, looked up, and asked, "Why?"

"I just need to talk to you. Can you come outside for a minute?"

"Kathy, what are we doing?" Linda looked back longingly at the lovely plate of food she had just walked away from to follow Kathy to the door.

"Well," Kathy tried to keep a straight face, but just couldn't do it. She laughed, "we're going to go for a ride in a limo with this man I just met outside."

"WHAT?!?" Linda turned around to head back to her table.

"Linda, it's ok. It's safe. The doorman said it's ok."

"I am not getting in…"

"I'm telling you." Kathy explained the story. "I didn't ask the doorman. He just kinda told me, 'You want to go on this ride.'"

Linda looked at Kathy like she had lost her mind. "Oh my God. You're crazy." She burst out laughing. "All right. Let's do it!"

As Kathy went outside to tell the man they were coming for the ride in his limo, Linda stopped to talk to the doorman. She wanted to hear it from him. He reassured Linda they would be safe.

The other Angel Mom and her daughter came outside about that time, and another Angel Mom came outside at the same time to smoke. Kathy called out to her, "Hey, come on. You're going with us!" All in all, six of the group ended up going on the limo adventure.

Meanwhile, the gentleman and Linda were talking about Arkansas. She told him she was a senator. "Ah," he says, "The Attorney General there is a good friend of mine."

Linda laughed and looked at Kathy, her eyes sparkling. "We're going for a ride!"

Just before they got into the limo, Linda stopped by the back of the car and said to Kathy, "Take a picture of me."

Kathy dug around in her purse to find her phone. Linda struck a pose and smiled for the photo. As they climbed into the limousine, she whispered in Kathy's ear, "Send a copy over to someone you trust, and send a copy to your husband."

"OK. Why?" It took her a minute to realize what she was doing. Linda had strategically positioned herself so the license plate would be in the picture. By sending the photo to a couple of people, someone would know who the last person she was with was if anything happened to her.

Linda was careful like that, Kathy was learning. The more she was around Linda, the more she realized the things she originally thought were odd little quirks were actually precautions Linda took out of fear of her ex-husband. It was easier for her to relax far away from home in DC, but even when she went on crazy adventures, she still remained on guard.

Daniel[1] took them on a grand tour of historical sites around DC. The Angel Moms shared stories with him of their kids and family members who were killed. But they also had a lot of fun that night. They cut up and laughed like they had not laughed in a long time.

They took lots of pictures of the sights all over the city. Everywhere they went, it seemed all the locals knew their host and greeted him warmly. He would not let them take photos of him, however.

"Why can't we take a picture with you?" one of the ladies asked curiously. "Who are you?"

He just chuckled good-naturedly and replied, "I'm FBI. You guys are fine."

After taking them to a few of the sights, their tour guide stopped at a bar. A shoe-shining man approached Kathy. She was the only one wearing leather shoes, and he wanted to shine her boots. Daniel smiled and encouraged her to let him shine her shoes. "I've known this guy for thirty years."

While the two men chatted, Kathy lowered her voice to Linda. "Get him inside so I can find out from the shoe-shiner guy who he is."

She sat down in the seat to get her boots fixed up. As soon as Linda and their tour guide got inside the door, Kathy asked, "How long have you known Daniel?"

"Aw, about thirty years. He's great. Great guy."

"So we're safe with him?"

"Oh yeah."

She leaned down. "What exactly does he do?"

He paused from his work and looked up at her with a twinkle in his eye. "You don't know who Daniel is?"

"I don't have any idea who he is," she confided. "That's why I'm asking you!"

"Honey, he is high up in the FBI. He is well known around here."

"So I guess I'm safe with him then."

Amusement played across his face. "Yes, ma'am. I guess you're safe with him." He finished his shine with a flourish, then Kathy went inside to find Linda.

Kathy grabbed Linda to go with her to the Ladies Room. As soon as the door closed behind them, Kathy blurted, "The shoe-shine guy says Daniel is FBI. Apparently, he is a big deal here."

"I know. That is what he told me. But I didn't know if I believed him or not!"

They joined the rest of the group. After taking them to a few more DC sights, Daniel announced their next stop would be the White House. "Are any of you carrying guns or other weapons?"

They assured him they were not.

Adventures in DC

At the next stoplight, he asked again if anyone was carrying any weapons.

"Why do you keep asking that?" Kathy wanted to know.

Daniel looked directly at Linda and Kathy. "You ARE from Arkansas," he deadpanned.

His comment brought a round of laughter from the group. He had a point, Kathy had to admit. Arkansas is well known as a Second Amendment state, and she knew Linda almost always had a gun on her. Just to make sure, she leaned over to Linda and whispered, "Are you carrying?"

"No," Linda whispered back. "I had to fly here."

When they got to the White House, the guards said there was something going on that night, so they were not able to go inside. If they came back the next day, they said, Daniel could give them a personal tour. The group snapped some photos in front of the White House, then loaded back into the limo.

The chemistry between Linda and Daniel was hard to miss. They joked and laughed together the entire evening.

It was somewhere around 3:30 a.m. when they got back to the hotel. The bar area at the hotel was shut down when Daniel walked them in all inside. Kathy made her excuses to bow out and go back to the room. "Take your time, Linda. I'll see you whenever you come up."

Kathy was just about asleep when, about a half hour or so later, Linda came up to the room and plopped down on her bed, giggling like a googly-eyed teenager. Kathy felt like she was in high school all over again. They lay in their beds laughing and talking until they fell asleep. Neither one remembered the last thing that was said.

They had their alarms set to be ready for an early breakfast meeting.

As soon as they woke up, Linda said, "Dang it! Dang it!"

"What?"

"He wanted my phone number, and I told him that if he was really the FBI, he could get it for himself!"

Kathy laughed as Linda groaned and buried her face in her pillow. "Ugh! Why didn't I get his number?"

They got ready and went to their breakfast meeting, then did a news conference with Angel Families. The next thing on their agenda was a meeting with Senator John Boozman at his office.

"It's such a nice morning," Linda chirped. "Why don't we walk over there?"

When Kathy agreed, "Sure, let's walk," she did not realize Capitol Hill is an actual hill. Both ladies wore high heel shoes for their meetings that day. Kathy's heels were three inches, but Linda wore spike heels. By the time they were halfway there, they deeply regretted their decision to go on foot.

All the while, Linda kicked herself for not getting Daniel's number.

"Are you going to try to track him down?"

"I don't even know his last name."

Just then, they noticed a sign across the street. "Linda, your prayers have been answered. Look across the street."

It read, "FBI Building."

Linda let out a squeal of delight, "Oh my God!"

"I guess it was meant to be." Kathy did not realize till later that Linda knew all along their route would take them right by the building. No wonder she was so enthusiastic about walking.

Linda sighed. "But we can't stop now. We're going to have to check it out on the way back."

"How much farther?" Things in Washington, D.C., often look much closer on the map than they are in real life. Their high heels were not helping matters. When they got to Capitol Hill, they realized they were still a block and a half over from where they needed to be. They trudged on and made it to their meeting.

When they came out, Linda asked, "You ready to walk back?"

"No." Kathy's feet were not happy with her. "We are getting an Uber. I am not walking!"

Once they got their ride, they were so engrossed in conversation about their meeting they forgot to watch for the FBI building. They had to rush off to another meeting as soon as they got back to the hotel (after they changed shoes.)

There were a total of twenty-nine Angel Families members in the capitol at the time, and they hoped to be able to see the president. However, so much was going on that the White House told their group coordinator President Trump would not be able to meet with them. They later learned that the information that they were in town was kept from him.

During that week, Linda accompanied Kathy to a meeting with the group FAIR, the Federation for American Immigration Reform, a non-partisan public interest group working to change immigration policies. Kathy had been in close contact with the group and was eager to connect them with Linda. The meeting proved productive, leading to discussions about Linda and Kathy working for the organization.

By the time they had been there for a week, Kathy was worn out. She had only been home a few days all month. Linda wanted her to stay over a couple more days with her.

Kathy was ready to sleep in her own bed. "Sorry, Linda. I'm going home."

She headed to the airport the next morning, but just as she was leaving, traffic came to a standstill for a presidential brigade. She barely made it to the airport and had to run to her gate. The flight had finished boarding. Kathy may be a tiny woman, but she can be quite insistent. "You've GOT to get me on that plane."

She made it home, but her luggage did not arrive till later.

Only a few Angel Families remained in DC. The rest had gone home disappointed they did not get to see the president. The ones who remained ate breakfast together at the hotel that morning. Linda came down late and joined them. The others finished eating and decided to go over to the White House and see what happens. They invited Linda to come along, but she told them she was going to stay and eat; the president would probably not see them anyway.

She was wrong.

This time word reached President Trump that a group of Angel Families who wanted to see him was right outside the White House. He had them brought in.

Both Linda and Kathy kicked themselves for missing the opportunity to meet with Donald Trump. If Kathy had not insisted on getting on her flight home, and if Linda had not stayed to eat breakfast instead of taking the chance with the remaining Angel Families, both ladies would have met with President Trump that day.

22 - No Slowing Down

"We have to find out how to get hold of Daniel," Linda insisted, almost as soon as Kathy's plane landed in Colorado. "Call the DC office and ask for him."

"You want me to call the FBI building and say, 'Can I speak to Daniel?' with no last name or anything?" Kathy asked wryly. "No. No way."

There might be another way, she told her. During their late-night grand tour of the capitol city, one of the ladies surreptitiously snapped a photo with him in it.

Linda asked her to send the photo to someone she knew in the FBI to see if they knew who the mystery man was, and, more importantly, how to get in touch with him. He looked like someone who had been in the media headlines recently, and that was their friend's first guess. They were quickly able to rule out that possibility.

They eventually figured out who Daniel was. Linda had every intention of looking him up on a future trip to Washington, D.C.

~ ~ ~

Shortly after their trip to DC, the Judicial Discipline and Disability Commission

(JDDC) issued a press release announcing the disrobing of Linda's ex-husband. On February 22, 2019, the JDDC released a "Letter of Reprimand and Agreement Not to Serve in the Judiciary" against Retired Circuit Judge Philip Smith of Pocahontas, Arkansas—JDDC Case #17-345. The document stated the allegations against him for improper use of court computers were "no longer alleged but proven."

As a result, he became "permanently ineligible to serve in a judicial capacity in the state of Arkansas." He will never be a judge again in Arkansas. He was, however, appointed as the city attorney for a nearby town shortly after.

~ ~ ~

Kathy and Linda did not slow down. The border and immigration remained political hot topics, and they spoke out at local events and did interviews at every opportunity. Some of their interviews later disappeared from social media and *YouTube* platforms because they were politically incorrect.

There were fewer occasions available to speak about Child Protective Services, but the subject was never far from their minds. They continued digging and researching, often behind the scenes. Parents fighting for their children frequently brought their stories to Linda, and she looked into them.

Linda texted Kathy on April 1 that she "just spent about two hours on a new case." The stories never stopped coming in.

Though she was no longer in the Senate, Linda worked with Arkansas legislators on getting bills passed. She remained bold and outspoken in advocating for what she believed in.

She was in the state house in Little Rock with her former colleagues when Senator Gary Stubblefield and Representative Brandt Smith saw SB 411, the "No Sanctuary City" bill, pass in early April and head to the governor's office for his signature. The bill prohibited municipalities from enacting sanctuary city policies. A brief version of Hailey's story was read aloud just before the bill went to the floor for the vote.[1]

Linda was a woman of action, but she also knew the value of prayer. In a text to Kathy on April 14, she told her how glad she was that she and Kathy forged a friendship. She told her she was praying for her and for America that night. "I need to do more of that — kneeling with my actions."

"Can you come out to Arkansas and do some interviews and spend the week with me next month?" Linda asked.

"Yes, I would love to!" Kathy responded.

They made plans for Kathy to fly into Memphis, Tennessee, where Linda would pick her up and bring her to Pocahontas.

Both Linda and Kathy were very active on social media, especially Twitter, Linda more so than Kathy. They frequently tagged each other in their posts and tweets, and Linda often retweeted Kathy's tweets, especially those regarding Hailey's story.

Linda was quick to post in support of President Trump, the Second Amendment, and pro-life issues like the born-alive bill. She relished the decline of *CNN* and called out politicians she saw as contributing to the decline of America. She posted news involving corruption within Child Protective Services. The topic she posted and tweeted the most about, however, was border security and immigration, with many posts from the group FAIR, the Federation for American Immigration Reform.

Kathy's story was never far from Linda's heart. On April 14, Linda posted on Facebook about a conversation she had with Kathy:

> I just got off the phone with an #AngelMom #AngelFamilies.
>
> It is 12:50 am. I care about the safety of our citizens and I know you do. Our problem with #IllegalAliens is huge. For

this family the cost was enormous. The loss of their daughter 20 years old and the [sic] she had a toddler that was left behind.

A financial burden from the entire situation and stress with having to be on court to try to get justice.

A travesty that some have intentionally turned an eye to the critical issue in America and Arkansas.

I am thankful we have a President who is trying to protect the citizens. We must help him in any way we can. The illegal alien invasion border situation is critical and sadly tonight I hope something happens to the Democrats in Congress that changes their hearts. Lord deal with them before another family has to deal with the heartache this family has gone through.

#BorderSecurity #IllegalAliens #EnforceLawsOnTheBooks #MAGA and #Safe

Not surprisingly, Linda paid attention to computers of politicians which became the subject of news headlines. On April 23, she tweeted an article about emails found on Anthony Weiner's laptop, "Judicial Watch: FBI Admits Hillary Clinton Emails Found in Obama White House[2]." One of her followers said this was interesting, to which Linda replied, "You bet it is interesting. The House of Cards falling? @JudicialWatch."

Kathy's social media tended to be a bit less political and more personal than Linda's. The first thing that popped up on Kathy's newsfeed Mother's Day morning, May 12, was a sweet memory from Hailey from 2013 which read, "I love you, hope u have a good Mother's Day. <3".

The next thing she saw was an article published by *Breitbart* entitled, "Angel Moms Remember Their Children on Mother's Day: 'The Hurt and Pain Will Never Go Away.'"³ Kathy's story was one of several featured in the poignant piece, written as "a tribute to the Angel Moms who mourn the loss of their children today."

It was an emotional day for Kathy. She sent Linda the link to the article. "I did not know *Breitbart* was doing that."

Linda was thankful for the well-done article that acknowledged the pain Kathy was going through, and she posted it on Twitter that night with the comment, "I SUPPORT #BorderSecurityNow. Two. #Arkansas #AngelMoms featured in Breitbart Article."

She received a blessing of her own on Mother's Day. Her son gave her a huge card saying he believed in her. His confidence in her meant the world to her.

She texted Kathy that she was going on a date later that evening. She didn't say anything then, but Linda was apprehensive about going. She had met him on Facebook, and he made her laugh. However, the closer the time came to meet in person, the more uneasy she was.

Kathy was getting ready to fly out to meet Linda the next morning and do some interviews with her in Arkansas. She still had to gather a bunch of papers and files to take with her on the plane, so it was going to be a late night for her. She told Linda she would be up, so she could call her after the date if she wanted.

She managed to squeeze in three hours of sleep before heading to the airport, but there was no word from Linda. After going through airport security, she had a few minutes before boarding, so she texted Linda. "So how was the date?"

It did not go well. Linda said she would explain when she got there. She was too upset to get much sleep herself, but she threw on some clothes so she could head to the Memphis airport to pick up Kathy.

"Don't rush," Kathy texted back. "It's a two-and-a-half-hour flight."

"I need that few extra minutes!" Linda still had to drop her dog "Puppy" off at the hotel she owned before leaving town. Puppy was old, blind, and deaf, so whenever Linda was going to be gone for more than a couple of hours, she dropped her beloved dog by the hotel she owned in town. There were always people in the office 24/7 who could take care of him any time she was gone.

Linda loaded Puppy into her red pickup truck and dropped him off, then drove to Memphis to pick up her friend. As soon as they got on the road back to Pocahontas, Kathy asked, "So what happened with that date?"

"It was awful!" She did not really want to go out with Clyde[4], but she went against her better judgment after he kept asking her out. He did make her laugh in their online conversations. Even so, she insisted they meet in a public place for dinner.

"I asked him for his ID. Then he started acting really weird, asking, 'Why do you want my ID?' I told him just so people know who the last person I was with in case I'm never seen again or if something were to happen." She laughed it off, telling him she could not be too careful as a former senator. He told Linda he did not know she had been a senator.

Kathy remembered the photo Linda asked her to take in front of the limo in DC and send to a couple people. She was not surprised she had asked for his ID, but Linda said things got pretty strange after that.

He finally explained he had gotten into some trouble in the past and had been to prison for a year and a half on a felony. Linda's gut twisted. "Why?" she asked, as calmly as she could muster. "What happened?"

"Well," he said calmly. "They got me for stalking."

The alarm bells in Kathy's head blared. She and Linda were well aware that the man who killed Hailey was eligible for parole after only two years and four months. What had this man done that earned him a year and a half in an Arkansas prison?

Clyde explained that it was actually a police officer he had stalked because the cop was dating his ex-wife. Because he refused to stop stalking him, the judge put him away for a year and a half.

Linda politely, quickly, finished her dinner, then told Clyde she needed to leave because she had to pick up her friend early from the airport.

"There was something very off about the whole thing, Kathy. I was so uneasy. I couldn't get to sleep when I got home."

"No wonder! That's just creepy!"

Suddenly Linda turned to Kathy, puzzled. "Where the heck are we?" They had been so intense in their conversation she completely missed her turn. They drove another ten or fifteen minutes before finding a gas station in the middle of nowhere so they could figure out where they were and get something to drink.

By this time they were laughing at how they went so far out of their way because they'd been talking and not paying attention to where they were going. They got back in the pickup. Linda pulled up a map app on her phone to get them back on track to their destination.

Suddenly, her phone notified her she had a text. It was the stalker, texting Linda that he had just seen them.

"Kathy, we are not anywhere near where he would have seen us!" She texted him back, "How could you possibly have seen us?"

He was on his way to pick up his daughter from the airport, Clyde said.

"It could just be a coincidence," Linda responded to Kathy's raised eyebrows. He had not mentioned anything about it the night before, though.

"Really?" Kathy did not buy it. Because of their missed turn, they were miles out of the way of any logical route he would have taken to the airport.

They stopped for dinner on the way to Pocahontas, then Linda took Kathy to the hotel she owned in Pocahontas. It was a late night of talking and catching up in person.

They discussed their plans with the Federation for Immigration Reform (FAIR). They were waiting for everything to be finalized before announcing that Linda would be working full-time for FAIR and Kathy part-time. Linda planned to move to Washington, D.C. Kathy would stay with her when she traveled there for the job with the organization, so they needed to find a place to live in the capitol city.

Linda had a flight scheduled to DC the following Sunday. Kathy was supposed to fly home to Colorado Friday morning, then fly to DC to meet Linda on Monday. They had several meetings planned and would be able to do some apartment searching while they were there.

They were both excited about the opportunity to work on immigration issues together with FAIR. Linda looked forward to going to Washington, D.C., and getting away from the corruption in Arkansas.

"Why don't you just fly to DC with me Sunday night?" Linda leaned across the table with an adventurous gleam in her eye. "Stay here and leave straight from here. That way we can spend more time together."

"I would love to, but my aunt is coming to live with us on Sunday," Kathy explained. "I have to finish getting everything ready for her. I don't even have her room finished yet."

They talked about ideas Linda had been tossing around in her head about possibly running for governor of Arkansas, or for the United States Senate. This was not the first time she had brought the subject up, but she never made a firm decision. There were pros and cons of each, and she went back and forth on the idea.

Linda had a passion for justice and righteous government, and she wanted to do everything she could to be a part of bringing about change for good. She loved her state of Arkansas, and she loved America. Where others saw darkness and gloom in Washington, D.C., Linda saw hope for government built on the principles embraced by the Founding Fathers—principles established in the Scriptures for truth and justice. She refused to give up and concede such principles to the corruption she increasingly saw around her.

There were other things Linda wanted to discuss, concerning what she had learned from a certain computer, but those were not things she could discuss in a public restaurant. That conversation would have to wait till they were in a more private place.

23 - "Nobody's Looking for These Kids"

Linda picked Kathy up the next morning and brought her to her house, a spacious brick home with a beautiful yard. As soon as Kathy walked in the door, she understood what Linda meant about the house not being ready to host guests. Signs of renovation were all around, and the floors were down to the subflooring.

"This is the room that will one day be a guest room." Linda showed a room filled with boxes and a desk and other office stuff. "Then you won't have to stay at a hotel when you come into town."

They continued their conversation from the previous night. They discussed their plans for the future and dreamed about the difference they hoped to make in DC.

Kathy noticed the security cameras all around the house. "I see you took me up on the suggestion to install security cameras."

"Yes, but one of them isn't working right." Linda indicated the camera outside the back door. Something was going on with it, and it was not picking up. She needed to get it fixed soon.

Kathy brought many of her original documents and transcripts from the DHS case with Brooklyn and Hailey to leave with Linda. They put them in the office next to Linda's bedroom, along with the case files from many other Arkansas families who asked Linda to look into their cases with Child Protective Services.

The plan was for Linda to make copies of Kathy's files, put a copy in her safety deposit box, then return the originals to Kathy the following Monday when she and Kathy were to meet in DC.

Even though she was no longer a senator, many parents recognized Linda Collins as an advocate who still cared about finding answers for them. The more she dug, the more people brought her their cases. Kathy's files only added to the huge stacks of papers in Linda's house.

"It's all come full circle, Kathy." When Linda and Kathy first started talking almost a year before, Linda had already been investigating DHS, the second set of books DHS was keeping, and the missing millions of dollars. When she initially began digging, she got nowhere. People all around her were being silenced on the subject. She never would have dreamed how close to home the stories she learned about Child Protective Services and the missing money were connected.

Over the next few weeks and months after she found her ex-husband's computer at her house, she kept searching and found more information on the computer. She told Kathy about things she learned that neither of them could have imagined in their darkest nightmares.

She found documentation on the computer connecting financial records with names of those involved with moving foster children around and trafficking them.

Though many children adopted from foster care are loved, cherished, and well-cared for, not all are. Some children taken by CPS are rehomed, sold as child sex slaves, used in child pornography, shipped overseas, pimped out, used for medical research, abused, or worse. Some of the children are sold on the black market via computer chat rooms that people must be invited to.

The names involved, Linda told Kathy, went to the highest levels of government, both on the state and the national level. Other names, both governmental and non-governmental, would appear prominently in the news cycles of the coming years. Documentation and evidence of this, according to Linda, were on the computer.

"All the while," she told Kathy, "no one knows to look for these children. They can go missing with no one reporting it."

They both knew that, meanwhile, the federal adoption bonuses continue to flow to the state and to the adoptive parents.

"Nobody's looking for these kids." Tears filled Linda's eyes. "The families think they've been adopted."

Once children are adopted out, CPS closes the file. They do not follow up on the children. No one ensures the children are cared for appropriately.

Linda had only one of the two computers she had seen in her ex's office, but the information she discovered on it was damning. She recognized the setting where some of the children were filmed—in Phil's courthouse office. She recognized the furniture. She found some pornography chat rooms on the computer and realized her ex-husband ran a couple of them. When all the information on the computer came out, she assured Kathy, many lives of people connected with this abuse of children would be destroyed.

No wonder he wanted the computer back so much.

Linda squared her shoulders and stood up straight. "This evidence on the computer, Kathy, will unravel DHS in Arkansas and put a lot of people in prison." Her complete confidence in the statement filled Kathy with hope.

Kathy already knew the answer to her next question, but she needed to hear it from Linda once again. "There ARE other copies of this, right?" They had previously discussed ways Linda protected herself.

"Yes," Linda assured her.

There was a complete copy of everything on the computer, which she had downloaded onto another desktop computer tower. Linda took one of the computers to a trusted confidant for safekeeping a couple of months before, after the repeated break-in attempts at her house. She confided the name of this person to Kathy, but told her no one else knew about it except for her assistant Rebecca O'Donnell (Becky). This was to be her "kill switch"—in the event anything happened to her, this person was to take the computer to the police.

There were other copies as well. Just as Kathy had seen with the photo of the limo with their Washington, D.C., adventure, Linda's practice was to make several copies of important things. She would keep one, then send at least two other copies to people she trusted. In turn, she requested the recipients of the copies do the same, and so forth. That way, there would be no way to track down all the potential copies in case anything ever happened to her.

She had done the same with the computer.

Besides the complete copy, there were numerous backup copies of various parts of the information on the computer. Linda had distributed the files with instructions for the recipients to make and distribute copies. No one person had all of the information. Linda made it clear to Kathy she had reasons for doing it that way, including the protection of the recipients and so that, in the event some of the information was compromised, not all of it would be.

It was an intense day of conversation and revelations. Kathy welcomed the comfort of her pillow when she finally lay her head down late that night in her hotel room.

24 - A Right Way and a Wrong Way

David Gutierrez and his girlfriend Chelsea arrived Wednesday evening and checked into the hotel.

Early Thursday morning, Linda picked up David and Kathy in her truck and they headed to the Conduit News Studio in nearby Jonesborough. They were scheduled to be guests at 6:00 a.m. on the Paul Harrell show, a popular morning radio talk show.

"I couldn't find my earrings this morning." Linda apologized for being rushed. The earrings she wanted to wear that day were missing. She searched everywhere for them before giving up and settling for a different pair.

This was to be David's first in-person interview with Kathy and Linda. He was a bit nervous, but he was thankful for the opportunity to talk about what happened to him. Linda and Kathy told him to simply talk to the host like he talked to them.

Paul Harrell put them at ease as soon as they arrived, then dove into the story of Sergio Rodriguez and the hit-and-run which left Kathy's daughter dead and David without his legs. David explained he had "post retrograde amnesia and thus could not remember the accident itself at all."[1]

"It was Election Day 2016, and I turned on the TV," Kathy explained.

"[Sergio's] face was up on the TV along with the election results at the bottom of the screen. It was that day that they actually did get him in to the police department."

"Where is he now?" Paul asked. "Was he eventually convicted of this?"

"Yes. When he did show up at the police department, [his attorney] was with him. He was not questioned, but he was given his rights and was booked in, and was released in an hour and forty-five minutes later."

Linda spoke up from her perspective as a legislator. "One of the concerns that we have in Arkansas, to be brought to light in the legislature and the judiciary, is that this man fled the scene. Why wouldn't he be a flight risk? So why was he ever allowed to leave the facility? It's very concerning. You've already got a strike against you. You're here illegally, and then this family," Linda indicated David and Kathy. "These two people here and their families are just—can't believe this. That's not the way justice should be! They should have kept someone that is a flight risk, and he IS a flight risk; he's already fled the scene."

"And my daughter," added Kathy, "survived for six hours after the accident, but two days later, it had been all over the news that she had passed away. I was with her when she passed."

She explained they did not know at the time whether David would pull through or not.

"So it could potentially be double manslaughter, double homicide," Paul interjected. "They didn't even know at that point."

"No," said Kathy, "and from what we were being told, what he was charged with was leaving the scene of an accident."

The show host struggled to make sense of what Kathy was saying as she spoke of her struggle to get any significant charges on the driver.

"It took until December of the next year before we got a second degree murder charge."

"What? Wh—?" Paul's brow furrowed in confusion. "That doesn't make any sense at all. I don't understand why it—it sounds to me like it was like pulling teeth."

Linda readily agreed. "It was for her; it was like pulling teeth. They had to stay at it. They couldn't quit. Had it not been for the families demanding and continuation of trying to get something done, I don't know that this man would have been charged. I mean, he's only serving eighteen months as it is for the life of her child and David's disability now for the rest of his life."

She turned to David with a big smile. "Although he's a fine young man. I've enjoyed my ride with him."

The host took the opportunity to address David. "What you've been through, you do have an incredible spirit about you, of perseverance, and I think that alone is a testament to just your character and who you are. Because I look at what you've gone through, and it takes a very strong person to be where you are today."

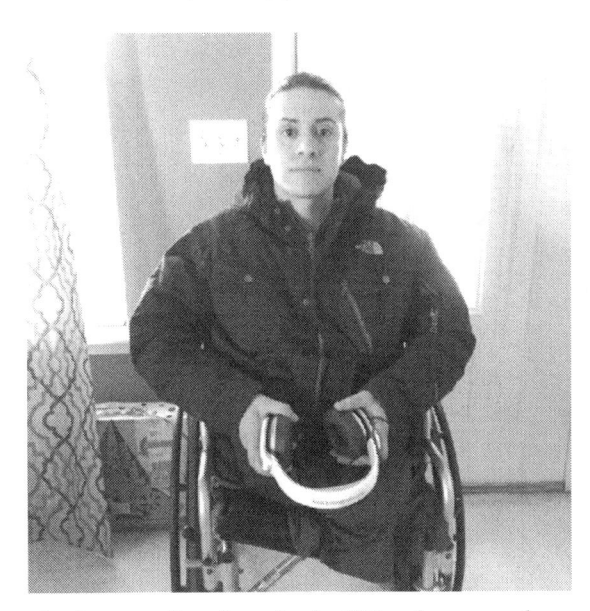

David beamed a huge smile of gratitude. "Thank you, and to me it's more of a strong testament to the power that God's given me and stuff, because first and foremost, He's helped shape my character. You know I was raised in the church and being a Christian, and to me, He's given me the strength more than anybody."

"Your last name is Gutierrez," Paul Harrell noted. "What's your family's immigration history?"

"My mom used to live in Mexico, and I come from California. I was born there, born in 1996. She came over here, and she went through the whole legal process and became a legal permanent citizen of this country. We're all glad that we were blessed with the opportunity for her to provide a stable home for us and a better life for us here in America, and, you know, we're proud to be Americans."

"That's another reason why this is so bitter in a way," Paul commented. "Because here you have a family that came here the legal way, and yet somebody who's here illegally—I mean, this was a thirty-five mph zone, and is the estimate that the truck was moving seventy mph?"

"Yeah," Kathy agreed. "There's no way it was thirty-five [that Sergio was driving], so I had fought to bring up a specialist here from Little Rock that came up and did a reconstruction of the accident site and calculated about seventy mph.

"I've heard a lot through being an Angel Mom," she continued, answering one of the main questions she heard from others when she told Hailey's story. " 'This was a car accident. Why are you fighting against immigration when it was just a car accident?' But that's not the case. I understand car accidents happen, but when my daughter was on the hood of this man's truck for over two hundred feet, and he never even slowed down, and he made that conscious decision to veer over into the other lane, hoping to knock her off—and he did—you know at that point, he made that choice, and as far as I was concerned, it was murder at that point."

Linda nodded her head and jumped into the conversation. "And he walked past a man screaming for help, and he chose to leave him there, and for the people of Arkansas, when you try to figure out, 'well, how do you arrest illegals?' There's a big difference between just immigration and an illegal alien that's here. They come here, and they don't necessarily want to be Americans. They don't do it right. But when you can walk past someone—and only get eighteen months—that's screaming for help and ignore that call for help, you could have allowed him to just die, and so what is the punishment?

"We've found through the legislature that, you know, Paul, they don't seem to get the same amount of time that an American gets when they do a crime, and that's just not right. It's just not right at all."

Paul asked Linda to elaborate on the eighteen months. She broke down the charges, plea deal, and sentencing, which would leave Sergio eligible for parole after serving just eighteen months of his sentence.

"Paul, I always make a statement: it's not an immigrant. Illegally here is an illegal alien. His parents," Linda indicated David, "came here to be an American."

"An immigrant technically has legal right to be there. An alien is actually—" Paul stopped himself, "I mean, you're right. See? I fall victim to how they try to change the wording, and gradually—and now you can't say the word 'illegal,' and now it's a bad word."

"Well, actually, now he is a legal permanent resident," Kathy interjected. "He was allowed to marry before sentencing. And that's an issue that we're having. I just got a call from VOICE [Victims of Immigration Crime Engaged] a few days ago that they're not sure when he goes to his immigration hearing, at that point they'll decide if it's going to be five or ten years before he can apply to come back. Because he is married and has a child, chances are he'll be able to come back into the country."

"It seems to me," Paul observed, "that with the whole court proceedings and everything that went on, that you guys were treated like *you* had done something wrong."

"We were," Kathy agreed. "When we went into court, we weren't able to ask for anything…. Anything that we asked, it was, 'No.' I don't understand it. The man was treated better than we were."

Linda had seen the same thing. "This family has shown me, at least Kathryn has, and I've met with David, visited with him for a good hour this morning too—is that they're not treated the same. The person that did the crime was treated so much better than the families were, and it seems like the system is upside down. We have to bring attention to that because we know we need changes."

Paul interrupted to ask her the million-dollar question, "Is this statewide policy, or is this specific to Washington County, and do you feel like the justice is—is this a political point of view in some instances?"

"I think obviously there's some political—as you know, you can't talk about these issues without politics seeming to be involved in that. So, I believe that we are Americans. Americans should go first, and if you come here the right way, we're going to help you, because we used to call it the 'melting pot.' We talked about that coming in today, and I want David to elaborate on that, because of what he said as well, but if you're going to be an American here, a proud American, and your taxes are paid to take care first of us, Americans first, we have to look at those policy changes. I think they've been ignored.

"I think the laws are there on the books," she continued, "and they've been good. It's just that we have ignored the law. Even in Arkansas, but not just Arkansas—that's at a national level. We've finally come to a crisis in our country, but David, go ahead and speak to that."

"On top of that," David jumped right in, "my family came over here, and they became residents, then citizens, and they gained their citizenship. We came from California. My mom, through the hard work that she's done, she's retired now, but she still works.... She was a single mother, and it makes me proud." His face shone with the honor he carried for his mother and his gratitude for the life she was able to make for their family in America.

"To elaborate on your point, Linda, what you were saying [in the car] about the checks and balances in the system, about the prosecuting attorneys having just about as much power as the judge. What are your thoughts on that?" David asked.

"That's an issue, certainly in the legislature, Paul, and you've been around this by being in the capitol and following when the laws are made in the off-seasons. That was an issue that we've had, and literally been snubbed and the insult that they think we need to change the Constitution if we want to have them prosecute and basically have more fairness in the way they prosecute. They have full prosecutorial discretion: if they don't want to prosecute a case, they don't have to. And it's heartbreaking if you're the victim or if you've been wronged."

Linda shifted the conversation. It was a subtle shift, tying into what they had been discussing, but Kathy immediately recognized what Linda alluded to in her next comments.

"Even the state of Arkansas trying to gain funds back in audits— they many times just would not prosecute, and they had the proof they need. They just were not going to do it." Linda slipped in the reference to the millions of federal dollars missing and/or unaccounted for by the Arkansas Department of Children and Services, and the second set of books. There was much more Linda had discovered by this point about the missing funds, but she had not spoken publicly about her recent research.

"We have to decide how we're going to handle crime," she continued, "and yes, the judges hear the cases, and I think judges are the ones who, if anybody's got prosecutorial discretion, I think it's them, and that's what makes it a challenge for people and families like this…. There was no fairness, it did not seem. Nothing right about that case."

They discussed bills under consideration which could make a difference if passed.

They all felt it was a great interview. Linda immediately posted the *YouTube* link to the interview on her Facebook page: "Illegal Alien Manslaughter in AR: Katherine [sic] Hall, Linda Collins & David Gutierrez Tell Their Story" at www.ConduitNews.com.[2]

She wrote, "I appreciated Paul Harrell and Conduit news for getting this story out and exposing crime of illegals in AR and families who feel they did not get justice because of negotiated deal by prosecutors."

~ ~ ~

Just after they left the interview, Linda's phone alerted her to another text from Clyde saying he had just seen them as they drove through the town of Jonesborough.

25 - Followed

"This is starting to get really creepy now, Linda."

"I know. It certainly is." The expression on Linda's face made it clear she was uneasy, but she did not want to discuss it further at the time since David was in the vehicle with them.

They dropped David off at the hotel, then Linda and Kathy went out for breakfast.

There was more on Linda's mind she wanted to talk about, once they were alone. "The governor threatened me," Linda confided.

"What? When?"

"He sent a message hinting about what happens to people who cross him."

"Geez. Did you tell your lawyer about it?"

"Yes. And a couple other people too." Linda rubbed her brow. "You know he's the reason I lost my reelection, right?"

"Yeah, I remember you telling me that. Because you were digging too much into DHS?"

"Yep. He picked his guy and threw his support behind him, and I lost." Linda lost her re-election bid by fewer than six hundred votes.

Linda refused to conform or be controlled, and that was a threat to established powers. If she did not believe a bill was a good bill, she refused to vote for it, no matter who pushed for her vote. If she did not believe in a bill, nobody was going to convince her otherwise.

Integrity in Child Protective Services and justice in the judiciary were huge issues to her. Her pursuit of answers into where money was going, and her investigation of human trafficking, threatened deeply-entrenched corruption and those with a stake in perpetuating the system. She fought with the same tenacity she fought years before for Second Amendment rights in the legislature.

She told Doc Washburn in a 2017 interview, "We need to keep fighting. We can't quit. That's the people's right that we have to fight to defend, and so we will continue to fight."[1]

In the same interview, she said, "I will support my governor when I can, but when he's wrong and it goes against the people and their rights, I will go with the people."

She and Governor Asa Hutchinson butted head a few times over legislative issues. When they disagreed over the budget in 2015, the governor made personal attacks against her and some other lawmakers. When Doc Washburn questioned her about it, she advised his listeners to call the governor's office to "let him know what you do and do not agree with. Be respectful. I wouldn't want you to do what's been done to me by a few people. I would want you to tell them why you don't like something, and I think that that's the right way to do things. And I would never do to him what I feel like has been encouraged to do to me in the public media, and I would want the respect—I think you're much more likely to be listened to if you're respectful."

The attacks hurt her, but she made it clear to Doc that she refused to respond in kind to the governor. "I really hate that he felt the need to do that…. I've hugged him. I've prayed for him."

~ ~ ~

After the interview with Paul Harrell, they went back to the hotel to crash for a nap in Kathy's room since they didn't get much sleep the night before. After their rest, Linda called Becky O'Donnell and asked her to come over to the hotel to meet Kathy. Becky was her friend and employee at the hotel, as well as a former aide when Linda was a senator.

Becky said she was sick, but Linda insisted she come just for a few minutes. It seemed to Kathy that Becky came grudgingly. She was polite but distant when they were introduced. *Is she jealous of Linda's friendship with me?* Kathy wondered.

"You don't look sick," Linda noted.

~ ~ ~

Linda took Kathy on a grand tour of the town of Pocahontas, population 6,600, before heading back to the hotel to freshen up and pick up David for dinner with Laura Abbot with Victims Rights Arkansas. Laura planned to interview the trio after dinner.

David was already outside waiting when Kathy came out of her room. "Have you noticed that we are being followed wherever we go?"

Kathy had not. "What are you talking about?"

"There's a truck that has been following us. Don't look over there, but did you see that truck right over there?" He gestured with a tilt of his head.

Kathy tried to look nonchalantly in the direction he indicated. "Yeah, I see it." She had not noticed the truck, but she had not been paying attention either. She realized then that David must have a heightened sense of awareness of his surroundings after being run down by Sergio Rodriguez's truck.

Just then Chelsea came out of the room. They loaded up into Linda's truck to meet Laura for dinner at Bella Vita, a quaint little Italian restaurant in the town square. The food and conversation were great as they debriefed from the interview that day. The conversation finally wound down almost three hours later. They headed back to the hotel to do the interview.

As soon as they were outside the restaurant, David noticed the truck that had been following them earlier. He whispered to Kathy, "Look right over there, on that side street."

A shiver went down Kathy's spine. Sure enough, there was the same silver truck she saw earlier. Like before, it was parked just far enough away that she could not make out who was inside it.

Linda drove them back to the hotel. They met Laura inside the lobby for the interview.

After Linda left the hotel, Kathy and Linda texted back and forth till late in the night. Kathy was amused that sometimes Linda seemed to think she was her personal secretary. "Can you get the phone number for the spa?" *(Spa? What spa?)* "Do you have a charger I can use?" "Any idea where the hair dryer is?" They often laughed about it.

That night, Linda needed a phone number for someone who was supposed to call her, so she asked Kathy to find the number for her. She found the number and sent it to Linda, followed by an angel emoji symbol with a halo.

Linda came back with another request. "And you find Daniel. We may have to invite him while we are there" in DC.

"Yes," Kathy yawned. "I'm going to sleep."

Linda was worn out, too. "I don't think I can stay awake. Night. See you in the morning."

"Goodnight."

26 - "He's Going to Kill Me"

Linda showed up late the next morning to pick up Kathy and take her to the airport. Kathy suspected she was late on purpose, and that Linda hoped she would miss the flight. Linda had been bugging her all week to stay in Arkansas and fly with her to DC on Sunday.

Sure enough, by the time Kathy got inside the airport, she was too late to board. She called Linda and asked her not to go far while she tried to book another flight.

Kathy made her way back to the ticketing area and texted Linda, "Ok I'm at ticketing where you dropped me off. No more flights until tomorrow."

Linda parked her truck and texted back. "Ok. I'll get you. When do you want to fly out. Just make your plans. Or wait to go w me to dc."

I was right, thought Kathy. *She did do this on purpose!*

"The ticket counter is closed," Kathy texted Linda back. "I'm on the phone." She was able to book a flight home to Colorado for Saturday morning. She carted her luggage to Linda's truck.

It meant they had another day to spend together. After a two-hour lunch in Memphis, they decided to go shopping before driving back to Arkansas.

They passed a jewelry store, which reminded Linda there was something she wanted to tell Kathy.

"You remember those earrings I couldn't find yesterday?" Linda asked.

"Yes. Did you find them?" Kathy asked.

"No. I went back to look for them again, and I realized that my mother's pearls and my wedding rings are missing. They're not in my jewelry box."

"Oh wow. Who has access to your house?"

"Just my dad and Becky." Becky and her fiancé Timmie Joe (Tim) Loggains, a retired prison employee, showed up in her life at the time she was going through her divorce. Until a short time ago, Linda also considered her to be a close friend.

"Could Becky have taken them?" Kathy assumed Linda's father would not have taken her jewelry.

Linda had recently learned Becky was writing checks on Linda's accounts. She had given Becky access to them so she could pay bills and deal with hotel finances when Linda was out of town, but there were checks written she did not authorize. Money also was missing out of her father's account. The books at the hotel were also not adding up with the activity she saw at the hotel. She did not know the extent of what was being stolen from her, but she planned to get an audit.

In the past couple of weeks, Linda had begun to suspect Becky might not be the friend she claimed to be, but, Linda said, "I really don't think she would take my jewelry." It was a mystery to her.

~ ~ ~

Linda stopped by the hotel to secure Kathy's room for another night. Kathy stepped outside the truck for a cigarette while she waited for Linda.

Linda came back to the truck with tears in her eyes.

"Are you ok?" Kathy asked.

"Yeah, I'm really good," she smiled and took a deep breath. "Daddy finally believes me." (She always called her father "Daddy.")

Linda explained she stopped by to see her dad when she went inside the hotel. She said her father just stared at her, and he looked very sad. "I'm sorry I didn't believe you about Phil, but I do now." He said pieces were finally making sense.

She gave him a big hug. She didn't know how to tell him how relieved she was that he finally believed what she had been telling him, but the expression on her face was unmistakable to Kathy. She loved her daddy, and his validation of her meant the world to her.

~ ~ ~

David and his girlfriend planned to drive home Friday afternoon, but when he started the car, the air conditioner would not come on. It was hot, and Chelsea was pregnant. She was not looking forward to the ride in the heat. They tried to book another night at the hotel, but the handicapped rooms were already reserved.

"There are two beds in my room," Kathy offered, since she had to stay another night after missing her flight. "If you guys want, you can just spend the night in my room and sleep on the other bed. We can all just leave bright and early; that way it's not so hot."

They took her up on her offer. Kathy and Linda went out for dinner, neither anticipating it would be their last dinner together.

David and Chelsea went out to eat as well. Before they returned to the hotel, they stopped at a store where David bought a tiny security spy camera. He was still uneasy about whoever was in the truck who seemed to be everywhere they were. Back in the room, he put the camera in a cigarette pack inside the cellophane, then placed the cigarettes on the window sill of the hotel room.

Sometime after Kathy got back to the room after dinner, they noticed the sound of car doors outside their first floor hotel room. They peered out the window and

"He's Going to Kill Me"

saw the same truck David kept noticing before. This time it was close enough for them to see the Oklahoma license plate. David snapped a photo with his phone.

When David later downloaded the security camera footage, they could see someone kneeling down and peering into the window with their hand up beside their eyes. The reflection from the cellophane made it difficult to identify the person, but it was enough to make them all uneasy. This was the only night the whole week Kathy was not alone in the hotel room.

~ ~ ~

Linda picked Kathy up at 4:00 a.m. Saturday to drive her to the airport in Memphis. The sun was not even up yet.

David and Chelsea left for their home about ten minutes later. Interestingly, the air conditioner kicked on as soon as they started the car. It worked fine ever since.

On their way to the airport, Linda told Kathy about another text message sent by the stalker. She had several from him during the week, and he was scaring her.

"This guy's getting really weird," Kathy agreed. "At this point I would be scared to say anything to him that he freaks you out."

"I don't know how to get him to stop contacting me."

"Maybe you should just respond to him and say, 'Hey, I thought I was ready to start dating, but I realized that I'm not.' That it's nothing against him, just 'I'm just not ready, and I'll let you know when I am,' then let it go at that."

"Yeah, that's a good idea."

His comment about not realizing she had been a senator really bugged her. Linda said she went back through their messages where they had been talking online before.

"Linda, it's right there on your page. It clearly says you were a state senator."

There were other things bothering Linda. "Some of the things he said make me wonder now if this man was maybe a set-up."

"What do you mean?"

"Like, maybe Phil had him do this."

"Do you really think so?"

She explained a few things he said which, when she looked back and re-read them, made her suspect her ex-husband could possibly behind this.

Kathy agreed things were not adding up. "What would be the purpose of that?"

"Trying to get me off somewhere alone." Her tone turned dead serious. "Because I know for a fact, if I ever have another run-in with Phil, and he's able to get his hands on me, he's going to kill me. There is no doubt in my mind."

Kathy sighed deeply. She wanted to reassure her friend, but she did not know what to say. Later, she would beat herself up for not taking it seriously enough.

The conversation turned to Phil's computer. Linda had been able to put a lot of pieces together with DHS, their second set of books, missing money, child trafficking, tying them with names and financial records she found on the computer. She had figured most of it out, and she would be ready to speak out about it soon.

"With the information I have, it could be dangerous for a lot of people in very high places and the corruption going on in the state." The steel in Linda's voice sent a shiver down Kathy's spine.

Linda continued, her tone very serious. "If anything ever happens to me, don't trust anybody in this state. Nobody."

She instructed Kathy to check her safety deposit box if anything happened to her, but she did not say where the box was. Kathy later kicked herself for not asking what bank the safety deposit box was in.

As they neared the airport, Linda put a CD into the CD player. Vince Gill's "Go Rest High on That Mountain" was playing, and Linda's eyes lit up. "I love this song! Do you know this song?"

"Yes, I do."

"He's Going to Kill Me"

Linda belted out the lyrics at the top of her lungs. Kathy laughed. Linda had the voice of an angel. The CD was actually a cover of the song Linda and a friend had recorded in Nashville.

It was beautiful to see Linda's passion, despite everything she was going through. Then again, that was who Linda was. She loved life and had the faith to believe things would get better. She was determined to get back up, no matter what came against her.

The lyrics of the song spoke of a person who faced down hardships. Their work on earth was done, and they were now on the mountain above with the Father and the Son.

They had no way of knowing how prophetic the song would prove—that this was the last time they would see each other in this life.

Linda dropped Kathy off at the airport. This time they were on time, but Linda was not taking any chances. Several minutes after Kathy went inside, she texted her, "Let me know that you were going to be able to take off or check in because I'm not gonna leave the airport until you do."

"I'm good. Drive safe."

"Did they take you in?"

"Yes, going through security."

"Ok be safe."

"See you Monday."

"Ok. Great. I arrive DC 10:10. I'll send flight info."

27 - Something's Wrong

Linda drove home and changed clothes to attend a political fundraiser Crawfish boil on Saturday afternoon in Bowman, Arkansas, to support her colleague, conservative Arkansas Senate candidate Representative Dan Sullivan. She texted Kathy about running into an old friend, Rendall Wallace, at the event. He was an old flame, she said, but she had no romantic interest in him. She did, however, have fun dancing with him after the event before heading home to pack for her late-night flight the next day to Washington, D.C.

Kathy was not able to make the trip to DC to meet Linda because of a family issue that came up. Linda met with the Federation for American Immigration Reform in DC to negotiate her salary and work on other details about her upcoming move to DC to work for FAIR.

On Wednesday, May 22, Linda flew to Arizona from DC to spend a few days with some relatives there. She met with several lawmakers while she was there to discuss immigration issues, but that was not the only thing they talked about, nor was it the primary topic of conversation. She went there to talk with them about the child trafficking through CPS she had uncovered. Children were being supplied for pedophiles and traffickers, and they needed to be stopped.

There were dark connections between Arizona and Arkansas, some of which would come to public attention in a few months.

Part of the reason Linda was in Arizona was to point out that the corruption she saw in Child Protective Services in Arkansas was by no means limited to one or two states. It is a nationwide problem, and Linda frequently worked to educate people about it.

Linda posted an article to her Facebook friends on May 22 about a DHS social worker in Iowa who was charged with lying to a court about a family and fabricating evidence. The case resulted in the termination of parental rights for the parents of four children.[1]

Two days later, Linda reposted an article out of Dothan, Alabama, entitled, "Police: Lab owner falsified drug screen test results to Dale County DHR."[2] (DHR is Alabama's Department of Human Resources. CPS and Guardianship abuse cases fall under their umbrella.) A lab owner was arrested on charges of altering and forging drug screens and paternity tests reported to DHR. As a result, many innocent families lost their children. She was later convicted and sentenced to fifteen years in prison.

Linda added her commentary to the story:

> I know of another case as well. It will make you so mad to know that this happens just to take Children away. Then to hear DHS say we do not have that information you requested in the file. Really? How convenient. And by the time information can get to proper location for help because the families run out of money, the child has been adopted and gone from you two years. I know all DHS workers do not do this but it is starting to look like a pattern and then when the

Judge in the case gives more credibility or weight to those DHS workers testimony, then just know your case is probably lost. The family and children lose.

Kathy texted Linda Sunday morning, May 26, to ask if she had time to talk about the upcoming show with Doc Washburn. She said a journalist and author of *The Definitive Dossier of PTSD in Whistleblowers* "Mike Volpe is doing a huge story" about Child Protective Services.

Linda texted back that she could talk "for a tiny bit. I'm outside but left my group." She called Kathy and they discussed the Mike Volpe story. Linda said she was going to her daughter's house on Wednesday, then she would be in the studio with Doc Washburn at his radio station on Friday. Kathy would be on the show via telephone.

Linda said she would be flying into Little Rock late Monday night and asked Kathy to call her Tuesday morning.

Linda left Arizona Monday night. She called Kathy when she got to the airport. Linda said she had a great time with her cousins, and she had some good, productive meetings with Arizona legislators. She would tell Kathy about them when she got back home.

She laughed as she told Kathy about her cousin's dogs who liked to eat carrots.

They also discussed the upcoming show with Doc Washburn. Linda was thankful, she said, that Kathy was not going to be in Little Rock in person because it may not be safe. "We are going to open up a whole can of worms!"

Becky O'Donnell picked Linda up from the airport in Little Rock and dropped her off at her house after midnight.

Kathy and Linda spoke on the phone Tuesday morning, May 28, around 11:30 a.m. Linda said she needed to stop by the hotel to pick up Puppy. She told Kathy she finally had a chance to go through her emails that morning, and one email in particular was quite interesting. It came from someone who heard their recent interview, and it had to do with Brooklyn's adoption and Hailey's death. "Call me back tonight and I'll fill you in."

"You can't leave me hanging like this! What did the email say?"

"Let me have somebody look at it before I jump to conclusions and I'm wrong," Linda laughed. "Call me back at 6:30."

"All right." Kathy sighed. She knew better than to push Linda to talk about it before she was sure. She would just have to wait. She had no way of knowing this was the last time she would speak to her friend. She would also never find out what the email said.

Kathy lost track of time after supper, so she was twenty minutes late calling Linda. Normally if Linda told her to call at a specific time and Kathy was late calling, Linda would call her saying, "All right, Kathryn, you've got to start paying more attention to time."

She dialed Linda's number at 6:50 p.m., but it went straight to voicemail. She expected Linda to send a text any second, saying she was charging her phone and would call her in twenty or thirty minutes. That is what always happened before, and Kathy had no reason to expect anything different.

Linda did not call back. Kathy tried again after a few minutes, but, again, her call went to voicemail.

She tried to reach her several times, to no avail. It was getting late, so Kathy finally went to bed.

She tried calling again Wednesday morning, but kept reaching Linda's voicemail. Linda had told her the only day she would be home all week was Tuesday, because she was leaving Wednesday morning to go to her daughter's house. Still, she should have been reachable by cell phone.

They had the huge interview scheduled for Friday with Doc Washburn. It was going to be an explosive show. Linda planned to reveal what she had found about CPS and the links to child trafficking. This was the show where she was going to lay it all out. Doc Washburn was not aware of just how big the show was going to be. He knew they would be talking about DHS and illegal aliens, but Linda had not told him how deep she planned to go.

Kathy sent a text to Linda, "Hey, don't forget about Doc Washburn." Surely, Kathy thought, she will want to talk about the show.

There was no response.

Kathy checked Linda's social media, but could not see where she had been online since Tuesday. It was highly unusual for Linda not to be on any social media site for long; she posted frequently on Twitter and Facebook.

The last time she posted anything on Twitter was on Sunday, May 26. While she was still in Arizona, Linda retweeted an article exposing NXIVM sex cult traffickers at 2:00 p.m., followed by a retweet of an article from FAIR at 8:00 p.m. about President Trump enforcing a provision of immigration law. At 9:36 that night, Linda posted a news story from her home state about floodwaters reaching homes along the Arkansas River.

Just before midnight, Linda posted this reply to a friend's tweet, "Power. You bet. Like a lightning bolt that strikes. A single bolt reminds me of the Almighty Power of God."

The comment was Linda's final interaction on Twitter.

Kathy searched Facebook and found a couple posts sent to "friends only." One was on Monday, May 27. Always the pro-life warrior, Linda reposted an article from *Lifenews.com* entitled, "California Senate Passes Bill Mandating Free Abortions at All Colleges and Universities."

Her final post on social media was to Facebook on Tuesday, May 28. She posted local artists Lee Street Lyrical singing, "Gulf Coast Highway," a melancholy country song about a couple finishing their life's work and catching the wing of a bird to fly away to heaven. Linda commented, "Beautiful voice."

Since then, Kathy was not able to find any other social media activity; this was unlike Linda.

Kathy sent a message to her friend Beth[3] in Arkansas asking if she had heard anything from Linda. She had not. "Something's wrong. She is not responding. She hasn't been on any social media, and I am really worried."

Beth said she would make some phone calls and get back with Kathy.

She called Kathy on Thursday. She was not able to reach Linda or find out anything. "Well, there is a lot of flooding going on right now," she offered.

News reports showed significant flooding of the Black River, and it impacted the region around Pocahontas. Linda had her hotel business, and she had a couple other houses being renovated, besides the home she lived in. Kathy conceded the possibility that Linda got busy sandbagging and was not reachable, but the more she thought about it, she did not think that was the case. Linda typically would have at least posted something online saying she'd been sandbagging all day, or the water levels were at whatever level they were. Kathy's apprehension grew.

Doc Washburn called Kathy later that morning. Their big show with Linda was supposed to be the next day, Friday, May 31. "Look, I'm sorry, Kathy. Can we delay this interview a little bit? We are swamped trying to get information out about this flood as a public service. It's all anyone is talking about right now."[4]

The National Guard had been called in, and that was the news everyone was interested in at the moment. Doc had not had time to reach out to Linda, but he wanted to reschedule their show for the following Friday.

"I haven't been able to reach Linda, Doc, and I'm really, really worried. Nobody is hearing from her, and she is not on social networking." Again, she conceded that the flooding could possibly explain it.

"I will get with you and Linda the first of the week, but we'll do the show for sure next Friday."

"OK. I'll keep trying to reach her to let her know."

She immediately sent a text message to Linda. "Hey lady. Doc Washburn called me. Because of [flooding] he had asked us to do next Friday." The show would have been on June 7. There was no response to her text.

She called Beth again on Saturday. "There is still nothing. Her phone is still going to voicemail." She had a gut feeling something was very wrong, but it was difficult to do anything from nine hundred miles away.

Kathy wanted to call Linda's hotel and talk to her father, Benny Collins, but she didn't want to upset him or worry him unnecessarily. He was ninety-four years old, but he still worked at the hotel every day, doing maintenance and fixing things. Linda had been worried about him because his blood pressure had been getting high. Kathy wrestled with herself about calling the hotel. Ultimately, she decided to wait.

Meanwhile, Linda's father was concerned as well. He and Linda's son Butch Smith looked for her. They went to Linda's house several times, but she did not appear to be home. Once, they saw Becky O'Donnell coming out from behind the house. She told them she had been looking for Linda, too, then drove away.

The gardener was at the house on Saturday to do yard work, but he did not notice anything suspicious or smell anything out of the ordinary.

28 - Kill Switch

By Tuesday, June 4, it had been an entire week since Kathy had heard from Linda. This was the longest period of time they had gone without talking since their first conversation a year before. She called Beth again.

"Nobody has heard from her." Beth sounded worried.

"I'm telling you, something is seriously wrong. I'm afraid. If I don't hear from her by 8:00 tonight—something, anything, she's been online or something—I'm calling the police." Kathy's stomach was in knots.

She was not sleeping well. She had a gut feeling things were not going to turn out well. It had been too long. At the same time, she thought, her family certainly would have said something if something were wrong. She would have heard something.

It had to be the flooding, Kathy tried to convince herself. *Surely, that was all it was.*

Her daughter and grandkids came over later that day. They were in the kitchen visiting with Kathy and her aunt when the phone rang in the office upstairs. She let the call go to the answering machine, but the caller was insistent and kept calling. Kathy went upstairs to answer it. The phone rang again as soon as she walked into her office.

Beth's voice was heavy. "Honey, you need to sit down."

Kathy knew immediately this was not going to be good news. "All right."

"They found Linda. She's been murdered. They found her about twenty minutes ago."

She crumpled to the ground. Her daughter heard her crying from downstairs and quickly figured out what her mother's cries meant. She gathered her children and took them home.

Linda's son and father found her body lying face down by the garage at her Pocahontas home. She was wrapped in a blanket and covered with a tarp. They called the police. Her body was badly decomposed, so much so that law enforcement had to wait for autopsy confirmation that it was, indeed, the senator.

"They are saying she was shot, execution style," Beth said.

"I need to call the police there," Kathy realized between her sobs. She willed herself to think practically. "There is information that I have." There was information Linda told her about her ex-husband. There was the stalker. There was the truck following them everywhere they went when she was there. She knew the police would want any information that could help them in their search for what happened to Linda.

Beth recommended that she not call them. She assured her the police knew who she was and would contact her when they were ready. They were just beginning to conduct their investigation.

Initial reports stated that Linda's former press secretary Ken Yang reported Linda was shot in the head. Yang told media that neighbors heard the sound of gunshots a couple days before her body was discovered.

According to *5 News KFSM*, she was found at the home she owned with her ex-husband, but he was not named as a suspect. "According to court documents, Collins-Smith requested a protection order against her estranged husband in November of 2017."[1]

Within hours of the news reports of Linda's body being found, Ben Simmons brought Linda's "kill switch" computer to the police. According to a June 5 Affidavit for Search Warrant signed by Judge Harold Erwin, "On June 5, 2019 at 12:05 a.m., Benjamin Simmons brought the above described HP computer tower to law enforcement authorities with the Randolph County Sheriff's Department. Simmons stated that he received the computer tower from Linda Collins-Smith a couple months ago. Simmons stated that Smith wanted him to keep it and give it to law enforcement in the event anything ever happens to her. Data contained within the HP computer tower belonging to Linda Collins-Smith may reveal important information into this investigation."

~ ~ ~

Paul Harrell invited Linda's former press secretary Ken Yang as a guest on his *Conduit News* talk show.[2] It was, Paul told his listeners, "a sad, dark day for the state of Arkansas as we are mourning the loss of Senator Collins who was found in her home yesterday, dead of an apparent gunshot wound according to reports."

He asked for prayers for the family, then said, "The good news is—she lived a life marked by the love of Jesus Christ, and if you knew her, you know that to be true, and death is not the end. Praise God, death is not the end."

It seemed for a moment Paul was going to break down and cry for his friend. He pulled himself together, took a deep breath, and brought Ken Yang onto the show. Ken said he was "happy he was not on TV right now" as he was "wiping away tears." It was a difficult show for both of them. He said Linda was a passionate Christian woman who was "unafraid to meet her Maker."

Paul described the former Senator as "highly relational. She genuinely cared about how you were doing, how your family was doing, how you were growing, how you were progressing throughout this life."

"She genuinely cared," Ken agreed, "genuinely wanted to know what was going on."

There were people in her political path who sometimes treated her very terribly, Ken explained. Some said vile, horrible things to her, but "those people don't know that, in private, Linda never said one nasty, ugly thing about those people. She might say, 'That person's being mean to me, Ken.' That's how bad Linda would talk about someone was just to say that they were mean. That just goes to her character."

Ken, who met Linda in 2010 and helped her with her political campaigns, said Linda was always very active on social media, speaking up about issues she cared about. They did not know when Linda was killed yet, but they knew her last social media post was on May 28.

As soon as they found Linda's body, Ken said, "Suicide was immediately taken off the table. State and federal investigators were headed up to investigate this as a homicide…. It's normal for state investigators to come; what's abnormal is for federal investigators to come."

Ken declined to speculate on details about Linda's death, but he said, "I hope a lot of questions are asked, and poked, and prodded. This cannot just go away…. Linda deserves justice."[3]

~ ~ ~

Later that day, just one day after Linda's body was found, information to the public concerning the investigation was locked down. Randolph County Prosecuting Attorney Henry Boyce requested an order for all materials and statements obtained by police during the investigation of Linda's death to be sealed. Circuit Judge Harold Erwin signed the gag order the same day.

Journalists later called the action "one of the strictest gag orders ever seen by legal observers in Arkansas history."[4] Doc Washburn and others called the move "illegal." The order was out before there was forensic confirmation that the body did, indeed, belong to Linda Collins and before there were any murder suspects.

Speculation as to what happened to Linda and why ramped up after the gag order was issued. Rumors and theories abounded regarding what she was investigating and the possibility that it got her killed.

Screenshots of tweets supposedly posted by Linda just before her death quickly surfaced and made the rounds on social media. One version said "Kevin's Post" at the top; it appeared to be a screenshot on a cell phone that came from Linda's Twitter page. It read, "I have found damning evidence that will lead to Hillary Clinton's arrest." It was followed by a news article reporting her death from a gunshot wound.

Another version was dated May 27. Posters shared a screenshot with the comment, "twitter deleted this from her page." The screenshot contained what appeared to be a tweet from Senator Linda Collins, District 19, which read, "I have information that will lead to the arrest of Hillary Clinton."

However, Kathy never saw those posts on Linda's social media. If they were there, she would have seen them. She had checked her pages several times a day, looking for any sign her friend was ok—all the while fighting the growing dread inside that all was not well.

Other people who loved Linda also paid attention to her online activity, hoping to find evidence she was safe, and they did not see any posts on her pages about Hillary Clinton either. As tempting as it may have been for some to believe, Linda did not post those tweets. They were fabricated.

Nonetheless, none of them knew, or could have known, what Linda knew and what she was preparing to expose. She was finally ready. She had put enough of the pieces together, but she and Kathy kept everything tightly under wraps. The former Senator planned to release bombshell revelations, backed up with evidence, about children being taken by Child Protective Services and money changing hands, but neither Kathy nor Doc Washburn knew everything Linda planned to expose on Doc Washburn's show the week of her death.

Over the next two days after she got the news of Linda's death, Kathy kept bringing up the need to call the police and tell them what she knew, but Beth repeatedly told her, "The police have your number. They know. They are going to call you. Just give them a couple days while they are finishing up out there."

Finally, Kathy called the Pocahontas police department and left her name and number Thursday morning. Moments later, a state police officer called her. They knew nothing about her. Contrary to what Kathy had been told, the police had neither her name nor phone number. She was very confused. *What the heck is going on? Why did Beth tell me the police knew?*

The police knew Linda had a friend in town for the week recently, but until Kathy called them, they did not know who it was or any details. "You were the one with her?" the officer asked.

"Yes." Kathy confirmed. She gave them all of her contact information and told them what she knew.

Some of their questions, she believes, were to ascertain whether or not she was telling the truth, which seemed logical to Kathy. They asked what car Linda drove her around in while she was in town. Was it the Camaro or Corvette or the truck?

"She didn't have a sports type car there. Just the truck. That's the only vehicle we were ever in."

They questioned her about things inside of Linda's house. "She's got security cameras all around the house," Kathy told them. "Why don't you look at those? That will tell you who was in her house."

"There are no security cameras here," the police said. They were told the cameras had been taken to Best Buy to be repaired.

A later report revealed Becky O'Donnell to be the source of that information. Becky told investigators Linda wanted the cameras removed because they were not staying charged. She said her boyfriend Tim Loggains took the cameras down.[5]

Kathy was surprised. "No. They were there when I was there." She explained that the camera outside the back door had not been working right when she was there, and Linda had planned to get it fixed. The rest, however, should have been there. She had them up because she was afraid of her ex-husband. She would not have taken them down.

The police focused in on Rebecca O'Donnell from the beginning and questioned Kathy about her and the involvement of Rebecca and Tim in Linda's finances. They asked if she was aware that Rebecca had gone on a shopping spree on the Friday prior to Linda's body being found, and that Rebecca and her boyfriend Tim used Linda's bank card on the shopping spree to pay for things.

"No. Why would I know that?"

Kathy and Linda did not talk much about her personal finances. She knew Linda was struggling to come up with a big bond for the courts on her businesses, and she no longer had income from being a legislator. She knew Linda had been upset that Phil ended up with the properties which were paid off, while she was left with the properties under renovation and with remaining mortgages. Linda had to try to refinance them, without a job, in order to meet the judge's demand that she remove Phil's name within sixty days. Linda felt the settlement was unreasonable and the demands impossible. She was appealing the decision of Circuit Judge Ellen Brantley, wife of Max Brantley, senior editor of the *Arkansas Times*.[6]

The officer asked if she knew anything about Tim Loggains having power of attorney over some of Linda's accounts. "Yes," Kathy told him. "Linda said this was so he could take care of payroll checks and such whenever she was out of town." That was about the extent of Kathy's knowledge of Linda's financial situation.

The big question on Kathy's mind was whether police had looked into Phil Smith yet. She told them Linda's statements the last time they saw each other regarding her fear that he was going to kill her. She also mentioned the mercury poisoning a few years prior. Police said they know nothing about Linda ever having been poisoned.

They told her, however, they had already cleared Phil Smith as a suspect in Linda's murder. Kathy was surprised. Linda had told multiple people about her fear Phil was going to kill her.

What about the stalker? Kathy told the officers about the man Linda went to dinner with recently and the disturbing messages he sent Linda. She also let them know about the person in the truck who followed them the entire week she was there. She informed them that David had video camera footage of the driver peering into their hotel window. Though she offered to get the footage to the police, they never requested it.

Kathy asked about the files in Linda's house. The officer told her when they found her body, there were no papers or files in Linda's home. Neither Kathy's files nor any of the piles of case files were there. They were all gone.

Police recovered two iPads, two cell phones, and an Apple computer from Linda's home during the first twenty-four hours after her body was found, according to search warrant data.

They asked Kathy which cell phone Linda was using. Kathy said she bought a new larger iPhone recently, which aggravated Linda because it was too big to fit in her back pocket. Police asked Kathy to describe it. She said she would send over a video showing the phone from when she was there. When the police saw the video, they realized they did not recover her cell phone in the items they took from her home. It was missing.

Kathy told police about the safety deposit box Linda said she had, but she did not know where the box was located. She never learned whether or not the police followed up on that information. A search warrant was never issued for the box.

Police did, however, verify with hotel employees that Kathy was checked in for the dates she gave for being in town with Linda.

Shortly after Kathy's conversation with the police, a state police officer called her again. The autopsy report confirmed the body was, indeed, that of Linda Collins. Her gut told her this would be a difficult call to hear.

"Oh, God. Please just tell me that she did not suffer."

"Ma'am, I can't tell you that." His response sent shivers down her spine. "It looks like she was tortured."

Kathy wondered—was it about information on the computer? She could not help but think someone was trying to get information about the location of Phil's computer and what was on it.

Initial reports stated Linda was shot in the head, and an officer on the scene told a colleague of Linda's she had been shot between the eyes, execution style. The official report from the autopsy showed Linda was stabbed at least six times. Blood stains found in Linda's kitchen indicated she was killed in the kitchen of her home. Her body was wrapped in a blanket—her son's old comforter he had taken to college—and later moved to the driveway, where her father and son found her face down in an advanced state of decomposition.

Linda was murdered a week before her family found her on June 4. She was killed after Kathy and Linda spoke the morning of Tuesday, May 28, and was already gone by the time Kathy tried to call her at 6:50 p.m. Thus, her call went straight to voicemail that evening.

Linda's missing cell phone was never recovered.

29 - "We Got You"

Friends, family, and colleagues were shocked at the news of Linda's death. Condolences poured in from around the state and nation.

Senator Tom Cotton wrote, "I was deeply saddened to hear of Linda Collins-Smith's passing. She was a passionate leader who loved northeast Arkansas. I wish her friends and family comfort during this tragic time."

"If she could stand here this morning," State Senator Gary Stubblefield said, "[she'd say] 'you just keep fighting,' because she loved children, she loved the unborn, she could not stand injustice, she worked hard for justice."[1]

Arkansas Representative Charlotte Douglas spoke of her passion for the people of Arkansas and her hard work in serving people. "I think you could narrow it down to a couple of words: she had backbone, like no other legislator. It just absolutely took the wind out of me to even think about that she had died, and I thought, well maybe natural causes, and then deeper into the conversation learning that it had been what we are finding out a murder."[2]

"... it's devastating and makes your heart hurt for Linda and her family," said State Senator Bart Hester. "No one deserves to go in a way like that."[3]

Former State Senator Bryan King told *ABC News*, "She was courageous. She was undaunted. I mean, a lot of the behind-the-scene scenes of politics that were so bad, and quite frankly brutal, she would keep fighting."4

"This is what I will always remember most about her," said State Senator Missy Irvin. "She was true to her views because of the deep belief in God and in His words. She was a Christian and she wasn't afraid to ruffle feathers to let you know about what His words said about that issue."5

~ ~ ~

On the morning of Friday, June 14, Paul Harrell with *Conduit News Radio* re-aired his interview with Linda, Kathy, and David. They had no way of knowing at the time of the May 16 show that David's first interview with Kathy and Linda would also be Linda's last major interview. She was gone, but the things she fought for were not over. Thanks to technology, her words and message endure.

Her life made an impact on the show host, who told his audience, "A lot of people, myself included, still grapple with this terrible tragedy, the murder of Linda Collins."

He announced the visitation for Linda scheduled for that evening from 4 to 8 p.m., with the funeral service Saturday at 10:00 a.m., both to take place at Sutton Free Will Baptist Church in Pocahontas. There was to be a private burial service following the funeral for family only.

The events of her death were "extremely puzzling" to Paul Harrell. "Please continue, I would urge people who are listening to my voice. Please continue to pray for the family. Please continue to pray for the investigators, that they would be wise, that the truth would be revealed to them, and that we would have justice on this side of eternity, because we know that there will be justice regardless in the end, but we would hope that the investigators would follow the facts wherever they lead...."

He refused to speculate on her murder, though he found the gag order strange, noting police were not able to comment on the case.

"Please continue to pray for the investigators, that they would know the truth, have it revealed to them, and bring appropriate charges on whoever it is, that is still at large. Keep this in mind—the murderer is still out there somewhere."[6]

His prayers were answered later that day, at least in part.

Mere hours after Paul's prayer, a Fed Ex package arrived at the police station containing a thumb drive with surveillance video footage from Linda's security company, in response to a subpoena from police.[7] The security cameras were still missing; however, the cameras uploaded their collected data to the cloud.

The account associated with the security cameras was accessed by someone between 3 and 4 a.m. the morning after Linda's murder. Police believe that is when some of the information on the cameras was deleted. However, there was enough damning information remaining on the footage for a warrant to be issued for the arrest of forty-eight-year-old Rebecca Lynn O'Donnell.

Kathy attended Linda's visitation that evening. She had to smile through her tears when she saw the casket. Bright red. *Of course it was. Red was Linda's favorite color.* It was only fitting she be buried in a red casket.

After Kathy left the visitation, she noticed a car on the side of the road surrounded by police armed with guns. *What is that all about?* A few miles down the road, she got a phone call telling her Rebecca O'Donnell was being taken into custody for Linda's murder.

~ ~ ~

Police escorted Rebecca to a white-walled interrogation room where she appeared calm at first in her white tank top. Her glasses were on top of her head, and the dressy tan jacket she had planned to wear for Linda's visitation service was draped over her arm. The officers' first questions did not appear to ruffle her. Then they confronted her with information recovered in their investigation.[8]

"You're under arrest for the murder of Linda," one officer stated. "Do you understand that?"

Rebecca flinched at his words and blinked in surprise. She turned to the other investigator who held up a photo of her with a knife. Her eyes flew open wide.

"We got you," he said.

The first officer clicked his pen and echoed his words, "We got you," and threw his pen down on the table.

Rebecca peered closer at the photo and did a double take as the investigator closed the deal. "We got video of you. You didn't erase them all. We got you."

And they did. One of Linda's security cameras captured the scene in her kitchen just after a woman's voice was heard screaming.

"You can quit playing stupid now."

Becky's glasses perched on top of her head in the video. She wore a mulberry-colored shirt instead of the blue top she had on hours earlier when Linda's security camera captured her leaving the house after bringing lunch to Linda. The video showed her wearing the same red shorts. A small, off-white shoulder bag rested across her chest as she approached a tote bag with bloody hands. Her lips pressed together nervously, in and out, in and out, as she dropped a large bloody knife into the tote bag.

The bag already held one of the security cameras that had been taken down, and it was still running, filming it all. Randolph County Sheriff Kevin Bell later explained to *Dateline NBC*, "As luck would have it, the camera was pointed up toward the ceiling."[9] As Becky turned away from the bag, the camera captured a shot of lots of blood on the front of Becky's little purse.

Security camera footage showed her leaving the scene of the murder at 5:20 p.m. Police obtained precise location data for Linda's missing cell phone from AT&T which showed the phone leaving Linda's home ten minutes later, at 5:30 p.m., and traveling to a location around the residence shared by Becky O'Donnell and Tim Loggains.

Hours after Linda was murdered, an outside video camera captured what appear to be two people hiding under a white sheet creeping back into the house. Official documents describe it as one or two persons.

In the 3 a.m. hour after Linda's murder, her security camera account was accessed and much of the data was deleted.

~ ~ ~

Rebecca Lynn O'Donnell was booked and held without bond on charges of capital murder, abuse of a corpse, and tampering with evidence.

Her arrest came one week after the day Linda and Kathy would have been on Doc Washburn's show if Linda were alive, the day she would have exposed what she knew about child sex trafficking and the child protective system.

~ ~ ~

Kathy attended Linda's funeral on Saturday in Pocahontas. Her heart broke for Linda's children and grandchildren. She knew how much Linda loved them and what an important part of her life they were.

She wondered why she did not see Doc Washburn at the funeral. Later that day, she got a text from the radio host. "I am sorry I could not make Linda's funeral. I was basically warned not to go for my own safety." He asked if she would be going to Little Rock before going home. If so, he wanted to invite her to dinner Sunday evening and introduce her to Linda's divorce attorney Kathryn Hudson.

Someone from the FBI in Little Rock contacted Kathy and asked her to come by their office before going back to Colorado because they had questions surrounding Linda's final week. Kathy wanted to talk to them as well, so she and her friend Beth drove to Little Rock and planned to spend a couple days there.

The dinner was rescheduled for Monday evening, but Kathy took advantage of her time in the Arkansas capital. They met Doc and a legislator friend for breakfast Monday, then went with Doc to his studio to do an interview about Linda's death as well as Hailey and Brooklyn's story. In the interview, Kathy exposed Brooklyn's adopter as being an executive with Walmart's headquarters in Bentonville, Arkansas.

She dropped by the capitol building after the interview and ran into a senator who Linda had spoken highly of to Kathy. He asked about the week Kathy spent with Linda before she died.

Kathy did not pull any punches. "Linda said Phil was going to kill her."

"Do you think Phil was involved?"

Kathy told the senator the real story behind Linda's broken arm.

"I knew it!" He had long suspected Linda was abused, but she refused to talk about it. In her humiliation, Linda had spent years trying to hide the abuse from her loved ones and colleagues. Few knew the secret torment she experienced.

Kathy confirmed that the black eye Linda hid behind sunglasses did not come from running into a wall. There were other signs the senator saw which made him concerned for Linda's safety.

"Where is the computer?" he asked.

"The state police have it," Kathy replied.

The senator hung his head with a sigh. "We will never know what was on it. They will wipe it." He told her about another computer wiped clean of evidence by a federal investigator in a Fayetteville corruption case involving a former Arkansas lawmaker.[10]

Kathy later realized the former lawmaker was brother-in-law to one of her attorneys in Brooklyn's case who always seemed stall on filing things needed for the case.

30 - "Did I Fall Down a Rabbit Hole?"

The rescheduled dinner with Doc Washburn, Kathryn Hudson, and another colleague of Linda's was not until 5:00 p.m. The restaurant was close to the FBI office, and Kathy had a bit of time before dinner after leaving the capitol. She went in to the FBI office to talk to them about Linda.

Once she got there, however, something felt off. A woman escorted her to a little side room. Three other agents joined them. The woman made introductions.

They asked Kathy for her cell phone. She declined.

Kathy told the agents about the things that happened the week she was there with Linda in Pocahontas, including the fact that someone had been following them all week in a truck.

The agents took notes, but they kept coming back to asking Kathy for her phone. She told them she was not taking a chance—there were pictures of Hailey and Brooklyn on her phone, some of which she didn't have downloaded anywhere else. They were irreplaceable, and she did not want to take a chance on losing them.

The agents said, "We are professionals."

After the fourth time the agents asked for her phone, she said she would gladly let them go through the phone and get any information they wanted, but she told them they could not take her phone. They were especially interested in messages and texts between Kathy and Linda. Kathy certainly understood that. She wanted them to solve her friend's murder at least as much as they wanted to solve it. She had no problem with letting them see all of the messages. She simply did not want to risk losing pictures of her daughter and granddaughter.

They were growing irritated, and Kathy was now late for dinner. "I have dinner plans, and I need to go."

"Well, we have a problem with that."

Here we go. What now? Kathy thought.

"We have a warrant for your arrest, and there's a police officer already waiting on you."

"I don't have a warrant!" Kathy was incredulous. "I've never been in trouble for anything in my life! What are you talking about?"

Then it hit her. "Oh, wait a minute. There was that misdemeanor charge when my daughter was killed. I finished out my probation before I ever left the state and everything was fine." She referred to the time she was arrested for bringing out her gun at her home when thugs tried to muscle their way in to hurt Hailey. "I had reason to worry. They threatened to kill my daughter who was killed a short time later. I was in my own home. There was no weapon fired."

Police officers came in and arrested Kathy. They handcuffed her and drove her to the Pulaski County jail in Little Rock, Arkansas. They informed her the warrant was out of Bentonville, a city in the northeast corner of the state, not far from her previous home in Fayetteville.

She told them she found that odd, since mere hours earlier, she talked about the fact that a Walmart executive illegally adopted her granddaughter on Doc Washburn's show. An hour later, she mysteriously had a warrant on her out of Bentonville, the city of Walmart's home office.

An officer escorted her into the Pulaski County jail. She stood by a desk in a huge room with cells lining the sides. Another police officer greeted them. "Who do you have here?"

"This is Kathryn Hall," her escort said. "I picked her up at the FBI building."

"I sent word—do NOT detain her." The Pulaski County officer did not look happy. "We can't even verify this warrant."

Kathy breathed a sigh of relief. *They are gonna have to let me go. They don't have a damn warrant for me here. Why are they arresting me if they don't even have a warrant?*

The two officers went back and forth. The escorting officer said a superior officer said to bring her in.

"We're not housing her. We are not doing anything. How far is it from Bentonville?"

"Give or take, three hours."

"Tell them they have three hours and one minute. If they are not here by then to pick her up, she's walking."

They told Kathy to sit and wait. She was detained, but no one did any paperwork on her. No one told her what she was being charged with, or why they were holding her. All she knew was that someone in the city of Bentonville filed something against her.

The escorting officer left the room, then returned a few minutes later.

The officer who seemed to be the more logical one asked him, "Did you call them?"

"Yeah. They'll be here in an hour and a half."

The Bentonville police were already on their way to pick her up. They arrived at the time they said they would, and they drove her to the Bentonville jail. By the time they arrived, it was the middle of the night. Kathy was confused, tired, and hungry. She still had no idea why she was arrested, and she had not had anything to eat since lunchtime.

In Bentonville, Kathy went through the booking process and paperwork.

"Address?"

Kathy gave her address, which was in Colorado Springs, Colorado.

"You don't live here in Bentonville?"

"No. I don't."

"Repeat the address again." It was obvious to Kathy something was wrong. The officer seemed quite puzzled.

Once the paperwork was finished, a female officer called her over to change into jailhouse garb.

"What is my bond?" Kathy asked.

"You don't have a bond."

"What do you mean, I don't have a bond?"

"You have to wait and see the judge."

"When is that going to be?" Kathy was new to this side of the legal process. She was not prepared for the police officer's response.

"We have seventy-two hours to get you in front of a judge."

They took Kathy into a side room with police detectives and a recorder. Officers asked questions, turned off the recorder, talked to her, then turned the recorder back on. Over and over this went, till they finally sent her to a cell.

By this point, she had been up all night, but she was not permitted to sleep. She was not called before a judge that day, or the next day. She did not feel well, and her blood sugar was high.

She was not on the list to see the judge on the third day either. However, they called her to the front booking area that morning. *Good,* she thought, *they gave me a bond anyway and I am getting out of here.*

Much to her surprise, the attorney who represented her daughter's killer, Sergio Rodriguez, waltzed into the booking room to escort her to a back room.

"Why are you here?" she asked. "Are you still living in the area?"

She peppered Kathy with questions, and Kathy could swear she heard the

Twilight Zone theme song playing in the background.

It got worse. "If you need someone to represent you, I would only charge you ten thousand dollars," she droned. "You could make payments."

Kathy sat stunned. She was speechless. *Did I fall down a rabbit hole somewhere? What in the heck is going on?*

The attorney's comments went from strange to downright bizarre. "I even have a bail bondsman that works for me. You can call and set up your bond."

What? No. "I don't have a bond." The woman finally took her leave, and Kathy breathed a sigh of relief when they took her back to the booking area.

Two of the detectives from the first day came in later and took her back to the back room. Their questions made no more sense to Kathy than those of Sergio's attorney. "When did you leave Arkansas?"

What does that have to do with anything? What does it matter when I moved away? I have the right to live anywhere I want.

"What is going on here? Will someone please tell me what this is all about?"

The detectives questioned her about Hailey's friends that dealt drugs. Kathy did not know what they were talking about. She explained they had only lived in Arkansas for a few months before Brooklyn was born. Hailey went to school and work. She did not have anything to do with drugs until after DHS got involved and Hailey ended up out on the streets. Kathy certainly did not know these people the police asked about.

Finally, one of the officers said, "I'll tell you what. We'll go talk to the judge and get you in front of him in the next little bit here, so you can get some bond and get out of here—if you agree to give us your phone."

"I'm not giving you my phone."

"The thing is, we already have your phone, and this is the way I'm going to put it to you. Either you go ahead and agree to let us search your phone, or we're going to get a court order for it, and it will be signed here in a little bit, and we're going to take it either way. If you agree to just give it to us, then we don't have to go mess with the judge and disrupt him. We'll make sure that you get bond."

So that is what this is all about! "Fine! I've had enough of this. Take the damn phone. I've had enough. Give me the paper."

Kathy signed their paper for the phone and wrote down her password. She later found out that, even with the judge's signature, they could not get into the phone. It was an iPhone, and they would not be able to get into it without a search warrant. If she had realized this, she would have insisted they get a search warrant.

They sent her back to her cell. By this time it was pushing 5:00 p.m. on the third day. Kathy feared she would have to spend yet another night in jail. She still did not know why she was there. It felt like she was in a third-world country.

Not long after she got to the cell, Kathy was finally taken in front of a judge.

The judge looked over the papers in front of him, then addressed Kathy. "Mrs. Hall, considering there are eight felonies here—"

"What?!" Kathy gasped. She felt faint.

The judge read off charges of maintaining a drug premises in Arkansas, possession of drug paraphernalia and various drugs, and possession of methamphetamine with the purpose to deliver. She was being accused of running a drug house!

Kathy was incredulous. *This cannot be happening.* This was the first time anyone told her any of the charges, and they were impossible. "Your honor, I don't even live in this state. What do you mean I am running a drug house? What is this?"

"Ma'am, it is not me you discuss this with. It's your attorney."

"Ok."

"Just because you really don't have a past record, I'm going to go ahead and be nice. You're bond is going to be twenty-five thousand dollars."

She could not believe her ears. Twenty-five thousand dollars was the same amount of bond they gave the man who killed her daughter.

As she exited the courtroom, the judge slipped in a dig. "Huh. You don't live in this state. Good luck on getting a bondsman."

What the hell is going on here?

She got back to the unit and was finally able to call her husband to tell him about the bond. It was time for lights out on the unit right after that. Kathy was exhausted. She felt terrible, and her blood sugar was high. She fell asleep almost immediately.

She awoke to a police officer telling her to get up. She'd made bond.

They did not give her cell phone back until two months later, and things had been erased off of it, including some of the messages and texts between her and Linda. She was later able to retrieve from the cloud most of what was erased. At least, she hoped she got it all back. She could not be sure.

Kathy walked out the doors of the jail and saw one of Hailey's best friends waiting for her. "Get in." She drove her along all kinds of back roads to get Kathy out of Bentonville and back to Little Rock, where she took her straight to the airport. Kathy boarded the first available flight home to Colorado. She could not leave the state fast enough.

By the time she checked her blood sugar, it was dangerously high.

The whole time she was detained, people were looking for her. Her family, Doc Washburn, Linda's attorney, and senators alike searched for her, but no one could find her anywhere. When the attorney finally found Kathy's name saying she had been arrested, the website stated she was arrested in Benton County, not Little Rock, where she was actually arrested.

The charges were bogus, and Kathy was easily able to prove it. She was accused of running a drug house in Arkansas with some other people. Not only had she never been involved with illicit drugs in Arkansas or any other state, but at the time this was supposed to have happened, Kathy and her family were living in Colorado. She produced documentation showing when they moved out of Arkansas, including the rental of two moving trucks and moving expenses for the November 2017 trek.

She also had the lease for the Colorado house and evidence of living there during the time she allegedly ran the imaginary drug house in Arkansas.

Once she left Arkansas, she did not return except for the sentencing hearing for Sergio Rodriguez, two visits with Linda, and Linda's funeral.

She had to return to Bentonville for court on the felonies—eight charges which diminished to three charges by the first hearing. Eventually all of the manufactured charges were completely dropped "for good cause." It all went away as mysteriously as it appeared.

31 - Trafficking and Fraud

Rebecca O'Donnell was arraigned on Tuesday, July 30, 2019. Prosecutors announced they would be seeking the death penalty for Senator Linda Collins's murder. O'Donnell entered a plea of not guilty.

~ ~ ~

Kathy lost her best friend and closest ally in fighting for justice for her family. Despite her pain, she continued to speak out, undeterred. She had made a promise to never stop fighting for Hailey and Brooklyn. Instead of letting Linda's tragic murder stop her, it made Kathy all the more determined to keep going. There was much more at stake here than one or two families. What she and Linda worked for impacts hundreds of thousands of people all across America.

The lives of Hailey and Linda on earth ended, but Kathy vowed to never let their voices be silenced. When opportunities arose for Kathy to tell their stories, she seized them.

She spoke with family advocate Seraphim (Raymond) Schwab on his *YouTube* show, "We Hold These Truths," on August 29, 2019.[1] Seraphim understood some of the trauma she experienced with CPS because he, too, had his children taken by the state of Kansas, the state where agency spokesperson Theresa Freed admitted that "substantiated findings account for only 4 percent of the removals the agency handles."[2] After a long, hard battle—and a hunger strike on the steps of the Kansas State Capitol—the Schwabs got their children back home.[3]

Kathy told the host the story of the social worker showing up at their home out of the blue and seizing her granddaughter Brooklyn when her daughter was away for a weekend visit with cousins. Naively, Kathy said, "I was still under the impression that, when we got into court, everything would be explained, and Brooklyn would be brought right back home. I had no idea what was about to happen."

Her husband Jeff felt the same way at the time. "The police are there. Give them the baby, and she'll be right home." But Brooklyn never came home. They also lost Hailey in the process, a process involving a great deal of fraud on the part of DCS.

After telling the tragic story of Hailey's death, Kathy told Schwab how she and Senator Linda Collins-Smith connected and worked together on illegal immigration and Child Protective Services issues.

Seraphim brought up Linda's divorce and the fact that Judge Phil Smith was removed from the bench. He asked, "What kind of things did she [Linda] believe he was engaging in?"

With a deep sigh, Kathy opened up. "Well, she believed that he was engaging with things with underage minors—sexual type things. She'd been looking not only into my case with DHS, but there was a lot of money missing from DHS that she'd been trying to locate. There was a lot of corrupt legislators in Arkansas. There were some other cases that some other children had been removed, and they don't know if they're dead or alive and where they've gone to."

Kathy said she wanted Linda to get justice. "She was a very honest woman. She was a very spiritual woman. She believed in doing the right thing when it came down to all the corruption and the children being removed from the families, and I believe it's part of why she was killed."

She and Linda had planned to talk a great deal about DHS in their next interview, but they didn't make it that far because Linda was murdered. "I know that she was fighting for me, and I'm going to fight for her. I just want to make sure the right people go to jail for this crime of killing her.

"My honest opinion is, and she had told me just days before she was killed, that if anything were to happen to her, that it would be for her ex-husband and the DHS issues. And I believe that."

Seraphim empathized with Kathy's grief. He was sorry she had not been able to make more progress on the CPS issues.

Kathy corrected him. Without mentioning the computer Linda ended up with or anything Linda had discovered in her research, she said, "She's made more progress than you think she has. I honestly believe that everything will get out there."

In another interview a couple months later, Kathy went deeper. She spoke with Brian Shilhavy on the *Medical Kidnap Show* on November 10, 2019.[4] Before the end of her term as Senator, Linda had been looking into a second set of books DHS had. "She had come across some information during all of this, that she believed she had figured out where a lot of the money had been going to and how it had been being moved." She said she could not go into details at the time because of an ongoing investigation.

"I believe she had proof of all of it before her death. She had uncovered a lot of information that came right back into her own home and was really struggling with it. Even before she had taken my case on, she had started discovering things that were going on and was having issues with the Department of Human Services and money and children being moved around. That's about when she lost the reelection bid that she had in. They pretty much got her out of office."

What Linda discovered with regards to the connection between CPS and child trafficking was "devastating to her." She cared deeply about the children, but, Kathy told the host, "nobody wants this to come out."

Attorneys involved with Brooklyn's case, she said, told her "children were being produced on demand."

When she mentioned Linda had been in Arizona right before her death, Brian brought up the recent arrest of an Arizona government official for running an illegal adoption business.

"I do know that she was discussing [Child Protective Services] with some lawmakers there, along with immigration issues," Kathy told him, "but mostly it was to do with child trafficking that was going on that she had uncovered. I can't give you specific names of who she spoke with, but there were different ones from Arizona."

Brian has seen a great deal of connections between child trafficking and CPS. He commented, "The corruption in these states is so deep that it's probably going to take federal investigators to come in—honest investigators—to come in and bring these people to justice."

The connections went deeper than Kathy or Linda could ever have imagined. The Arizona government official Brian Shilhavy mentioned was Paul Petersen, Maricopa County Assessor, arrested on October 9 on federal charges including adoption fraud and conspiracy to smuggle illegal aliens for financial gain.[5] Petersen was also an adoption attorney licensed in Arizona, Utah, and Arkansas. The Department of Justice indicted Petersen for smuggling pregnant women from the Marshallese islands and selling their babies through adoptions in all three states. Some would call it, and have called it, a child trafficking ring. The mothers were often deceived, believing the adoptions would be open adoptions, and their children would return to them at age eighteen after being educated in the United States. They were not.

Kathy was stunned when she realized this man living over a thousand miles away had several connections to the very courtroom which adopted her beloved granddaughter to a family of complete strangers.

The adoptions Petersen arranged for the babies of Marshallese women in Arkansas took place in none other than Judge Stacey Zimmerman's courtroom in Washington County.

Judge Zimmerman was the same judge who refused to allow Kathy or any of Brooklyn's relatives to adopt her. Instead, Zimmerman adopted Brooklyn out to a couple chosen by DHS.

As Kathy dug deeper into Petersen, she discovered he had another connection to Brooklyn—a connection too implausible to be mere coincidence. Petersen and the man who adopted Brooklyn were college roommates. Both attended BYU, Brigham Young University—the flagship college of the Mormon church in Utah, and they roomed together there.

It was during Petersen's obligatory two-year missionary stint that he went to the Marshallese Islands, learned their language, and made connections which would later germinate into the adoption ring scheme.

Brooklyn's adopter later settled in Bentonville, Arkansas, with his wife where he climbed the executive ladder at Walmart. His old roommate had to make frequent trips to the area in order to facilitate the adoptions of the Marshallese babies through Judge Zimmerman's courtroom.

Judge Zimmerman received a significant donation, to the tune of thirty-six thousand dollars, for her re-election campaign from Walmart, from the very division where Brooklyn's adopter was an executive.

According to an investigative piece in 2018 on these adoptions and the attorneys involved, including Petersen, U.S. and Marshal Island officials have known of these schemes for quite some time. "Money — for the attorneys, fixers, birth mothers and others — provides the fuel that keeps the black market going strong, more than two decades after the abuses were first identified."[6]

This is big business, very profitable for those pulling the strings. It has much in common with the adoption and foster care industry through Child Protective Services.

An attorney once told Kathy, "These children are funding the state."

There was another connection, Kathy learned, between the couple who adopted Brooklyn and Judge Zimmerman. The Walmart executive also served on the board of a rehab facility to which the judge often referred parents in her courtroom. He was their assistant accountant, and was later promoted to accountant shortly after Hailey's death.

~ ~ ~

Not long after Kathy's interview with the editor of *MedicalKidnap.com*, Jim White of *Northwest Liberty News* interviewed her.[7] On December 17, 2019, she again told the heartbreaking story of Child Protective Services taking Brooklyn and of Hailey's tragic death to an online audience. "I promised her as her heart was stopping that I would get Brooklyn back and get justice for Hailey."

She told Jim she had not seen Brooklyn since Hailey died, but she found a photo on Facebook showing she had been adopted. "It felt very similar" to when Hailey died. "I felt like we'd just lost my daughter all over again."

After this, she found out that more adoptions happened in Washington County than any other county in Arkansas. Since Paul Petersen's arrest, Kathy learned that every single adoption Petersen did for years in the state of Arkansas took place in Judge Stacey Zimmerman's courtroom. This was the same judge involved in destroying evidence in the case of child sexual abuser Josh Duggar, of reality show *19 Kids and Counting* fame.

They discussed Senator Linda Collins' investigations into CPS which began "long before she ever met me, over a second set of books and millions of dollars that could not be accounted for." At one time legislators thought it was twenty-eight million dollars. "She said by the time she was no longer in office, which was only a few months before her death, that she had discovered it was more on the fifty-to-sixty-million-dollar range."

Jim interjected, "So when I call CPS—not every agency, but generally speaking—when I call them a money laundering, child sex trafficking cabal, I'm not very far off." It was a statement, not a question. "Fifty to sixty million sounds like money laundering to me. That sounds like big-time money laundering."

When Kathy and Linda first started talking, their conversations centered around Linda trying to help Kathy with her case. "We had no idea when we first started talking that this would circle to her own back yard, literally. She had uncovered some information that was tying her husband, who was a judge, to the Lord's Ranch, which associates with Epstein, the Clintons, and so forth. My honest opinion is [those connections] are enough reason that she's no longer here. That's my own opinion."

Becky O'Donnell was in jail awaiting trial for Linda's murder, but Kathy told the show host she was not convinced Becky was the only person involved in the murder. "There's just too many things that don't add up. She certainly couldn't have done it [by] herself, regardless." At that point in time, neither the public nor Becky's attorneys had seen the evidence against her, but reports were that her attorneys were recommending she take a plea deal. She was placed into solitary confinement. "They don't want her talking to anybody," Kathy pointed out.

She was frustrated the police were not looking more into Linda's ex-husband. She explained to Jim that Linda had been married to a judge who was since disrobed over pornography on his computers—one of which ended up with Linda's belongings after the divorce. Linda was afraid of him, even more so after she figured out some of the things stored on the computer.

"Linda had told me on the way to the airport that if she had another run-in with her husband, she felt that he would kill her this time. He had tried in the past." Police questioned him in the beginning of the case, but nothing came of it. Becky was arrested a week and a half after Linda's body was found.

Strange things were also happening with the judges on the murder case. Linda was killed in the same town where her ex-husband had been a judge, and all the judges in the district knew each other. None of them recused themselves in the beginning of the case. One judge died, and another later recused himself.

Henry Boyce, the original prosecutor, verbally recused himself from the case without explanation.

These things all brought up questions in Kathy's mind. Meanwhile, state police have whatever evidence is on the computer in their possession. They knew about it and where it was. Within hours of Linda's body being found, they had a search warrant for it and Linda's computer, which contained copies of whatever was on Phil's computer that ended up in Linda's possession.

What was on the computer, Kathy said in the interview, "was enough to bring the whole CPS system down in the state of Arkansas, I'll tell you that right now, to bring my granddaughter home. She was sold off. Other people's family members. It was enough to put a stop to it and take the people down that had been responsible."

It is as if the computer and all the evidence it contains did not exist. "The police aren't even mentioning it. Nothing about it," Kathy said sadly. "You see nothing about it in the news, and they have it."

32 - Twists and Turns, and an Explosion

Kathy woke up screaming from another nightmare. It was the same one she had many times since Hailey's death. In these dreams she saw Hailey getting on the scooter. There was always a sense of foreboding, and she screamed, "No! No! Don't get on it!" But she always did. Every time. The dream shifted to Hailey's perspective and she felt the glory of the wind in her hair. She thought, *Good. Only one block from home.* Then, there was only blackness, and Kathy woke up screaming, realizing again she would never see Hailey again on this earth.

Her best friend was gone, too. Becky sat in jail, awaiting trial for Linda's murder, but there were still details about the case that bugged Kathy. Too many questions remained unanswered. She hoped they would be answered in Becky's trial, which was scheduled for October 2020.

Linda told her Becky had fibromyalgia, which interfered with her ability to do certain tasks at the hotel like change sheets. *How*, Kathy wondered, *would Becky have been able to drag Linda's body from the kitchen outside to where her body was found?*

Linda's attorney told her there were no drag marks either. Kathy did not believe she was physically capable of moving her body. *Did Becky have help?* It just didn't add up to her.

Twists and Turns, and an Explosion

~ ~ ~

In another bizarre twist, prosecutors filed new charges against Becky O'Donnell in January 2020, accusing her of a attempting to organize a jailhouse murder-for-hire plot to kill Linda's ex-husband Phil Smith and make it look like suicide. Becky also wanted to make a former judge and a prosecutor on her case disappear—Judge Harold Erwin and Henry Boyce, respectively. An alternate plan was for Boyce to be framed for murder. A fellow inmate told police Becky tried to recruit her and other inmates to commit the murders, blow up her vehicle to destroy evidence inside of it, then hack into the computers at the Randolph County jail to destroy records of evidence.

The inmate told police Becky mentioned Linda being stabbed sixteen times, lending credence to the possibility that this was more than a fabrication by an inmate wanting attention from the high-profile case. Linda Collins had indeed been stabbed sixteen times, but that information had not been released to the public. Only someone with insider information would have known this detail.

Becky reportedly told several inmates that Phil Smith set her up. She told them where to find a stash of gold and silver coins inside Smith's house, which they could steal as compensation for the deeds.[1]

At the time, Becky denied the allegations.

~ ~ ~

During the 4th of July week in 2020, a mutual friend of Linda and Kathy flew in to visit from Arkansas. His visit only added more questions to Kathy's mind.

Before Linda's murder, Becky had called him to ask him to take down the security cameras at her house. He refused. He later wondered if he had been being set up to take the fall for the crime. Like many others following the case, neither he nor Kathy believed Becky O'Donnell murdered Linda alone.

He told Kathy someone threatened him after Linda's death: "We like you, but people who talk too much don't stick around."

He was afraid someone thought he had a copy of the information on Phil Smith's computer, and he was scared. His house was broken into. The thieves completely tossed his place, obviously searching for something. Some money was taken, but, because of the Covid situation, which was in full swing at that time, local police refused to go into his apartment to investigate.

He warned Kathy to be careful because there were also rumors of her having a copy of the information on the computer.

"Those rumors are unfounded, I assure you," she told her friend. "The state police, however, DO have the computer. If someone there just had the guts to come forward, all the things Linda found could be exposed."

~ ~ ~

On August 4th, a month after his visit, a couple of friends stopped by for an afternoon visit with Kathy and Jeff. They were in the kitchen at the back of the house while the Halls cooked dinner. They heard a "pop" sound. Jeff likened it to the sound made when pulling the air hose off a tire after putting air in the tire.

Suddenly, about a half hour later, the garage exploded. Fire quickly roared through the house. There was no time to salvage anything. The Halls and their friends narrowly escaped through the back door.

"If we would have been anywhere else besides next to the back door," Kathy said, "we would not have gotten out."

There were three more loud explosions from the house. While they waited for firefighters, neighbors franticly tried to put the fire out with garden hoses, but the flames were huge.

Three different addresses were called in to 911, sending firefighters to a completely different neighborhood before they finally arrived twenty-five minutes after the explosion. The house was a total loss. Their friends had parked their motorcycle in front of the garage, and it blew up.

Their cat and two of their three dogs did not make it out of the house. Firefighters found the cat's lifeless body three feet from an open door.

Miraculously, Hailey's cedar chest and Brooklyn's dresser (formerly Hailey's), which were in the front room next to the garage, were not destroyed. Though the ceiling collapsed in that room, there was not even a smell of smoke on the cedar chest or dresser, or their contents. "It was," Kathy said with a grateful heart, "straight up divine intervention."

Two eyewitnesses said they saw a man by the gas meter on the side of the house by the garage a half hour before the explosion. That is where the fire began. The man was dressed in a t-shirt and khaki shorts, wearing a baseball cap. They assumed it was simply someone reading the meter. However, that region no longer has meter readers. The gas usage is monitored digitally.

The flames had barely gone out by the time the gas company arrived and dug out all the gas lines and meter from the house. However, no cause of the fire was ever officially identified.

To this day, Kathy wonders if the explosion happened because of the rumors regarding her having a copy of what was on Phil Smith's computer. She has no doubt someone was trying to silence her.

~ ~ ~

Just over 24 hours later, on August 6, 2020, Rebecca O'Donnell made what media called a "bombshell plea,"[2] confessing to the murder of Linda Collins in exchange for prosecutors taking the death penalty off the table. She told the judge, "I went to Linda's house, and I intentionally killed her and then hid the body." She also pleaded "no contest" to two counts of solicitation to commit capital murder.

She was sentenced to forty years for the capital murder of Senator Linda Collins, three years for the charge of abuse of a corpse, and fourteen years for the charges of solicitation to commit murder.

The family of Linda Collins released a public statement concerning the confession and sentencing:

Today our family has found swift justice by way of a plea deal. We know that there will be some that will not be satisfied with that outcome today. And we realize that whatever punishment [O'Donnell] receives it will never be enough .... It will never bring my Grandpa's daughter back or my Mother back or our children's grandmother back. No amount of punishment will ever fill that void that [O'Donnell] made in our lives the day she killed our mother.

Today we find some shred of peace that Rebecca O'Donnell will be put away in prison for a very long time unable to hurt anyone else. If my Mother was here today I have no doubt that she would quote the Bible and tell us that we can find peace in God.[3]

Kathy could not believe the investigation into Linda's murder was ending that day. Her first thought when she heard the news was that someone had gotten to Becky. She did not, and does not, believe that Becky could have been the only one involved in killing Linda Collins.

Because Rebecca O'Donnell was listed as a violent offender, she is required to serve at least eighty percent of her sentence before being eligible for parole.

Unfortunately, as Kathy learned after her daughter was killed, some convicted criminals in the state of Arkansas may be eligible for parole after serving only a fraction of the time to which they are sentenced. Though Hailey's killer Sergio Rodriguez was sentenced to seventeen years in prison in 2018, he came up before the parole board just over a week after Becky O'Donnell's plea deal.

As a Senator, Linda Collins-Smith had advocated for truth in sentencing, because of cases like this one. Somehow, the state of Arkansas listed Rodriguez as a "non-violent" offender for his manslaughter and battery convictions, making him eligible for parole after serving less than two years of his seventeen-year sentence. She argued there was no "truth" in these kinds of sentences, leaving victims further victimized.

Kathy Hall joined David Gutierrez in Little Rock, Arkansas, in August 2020 for Rodriguez's parole board hearing, just a week and a half after her house blew up. They were joined by Doc Washburn, Linda's attorney Kathryn Hudson, and Dee Ingle—member of Parents of Murdered Children as well as a part of Angel Families whose sister was killed by an illegal alien. Hailey's father Tom King joined the meeting via Skype.

David told the parole board about the coldness Rodriguez continued to display, reminiscent of the same callousness he showed when he did not slow down once Hailey flew up onto the hood of his truck, and kept going while dragging David's body underneath his truck, ignoring his cries for help when he finally stopped. Because of his lack of remorse, David told the parole board he withdrew his forgiveness he had offered Sergio in the sentencing hearing.

The parole board had the option to approve Sergio's request for parole or to reject it for either a one-year period or a two-year period. Two weeks after the hearing, the board notified Kathy and David he would remain in prison for another two years. Kathy realized they would have to relive Hailey's death every year or two years until Sergio is released or until his sentence is completed.

They still struggled to understand what happened that night in Fayetteville. On November 7, 2021, five years after the hit-and-run, Kathy and David sent a letter to

Sergio asking him for an explanation. All David wanted from him was an apology or some sign of remorse. They desperately wanted him to help them understand why he ran over Hailey and David and did not stop.

Sergio's only response to their heartfelt letter was to block them from contacting him.

~ ~ ~

Arkansas State Police unsealed and released hundreds of pages from their investigation files on Linda's murder to *ABC News* and other media outlets on Tuesday, December 14, 2021, in response to requests from media filed the day after Rebecca O'Donnell's confession of guilt more than a year earlier.

On the same day the data was released, Kathy received devastating news. Osmin David Gutierrez became the second victim of illegal alien Sergio Rodriguez to succumb to injuries sustained in the hit-and-run. He was twenty-five years old. Before he and his scooter were dragged underneath the pickup truck five years earlier, David had been the picture of health. The assault on his body took its toll, and his valiant battle for justice was now over.

Arkansas prosecutors told Kathy they would not be able to charge Rodriguez with David's murder because it would be called "double jeopardy." According to three attorneys and a judge Kathy spoke with about the case, double jeopardy would not apply. Charges are often upgraded. The previous case never went to trial; he pleaded guilty.

The state of Arkansas has thus far refused to seek a murder charge in David's death.

~ ~ ~

Twists and Turns, and an Explosion

Sergio became eligible for parole again in 2022. Kathy again traveled to Little Rock to appear before the parole board to argue for the continued imprisonment of her daughter's killer. Hailey's father Tom flew in as well. David's older brother made the drive from Fayetteville to be his brother's voice at the August 17 hearing.

The heavens themselves seemed to be weeping for the families of the victims on that gray, gloomy, rainy day.

The families were strengthened by others who came to stand with them in front of the parole board, including Dee, an Angel Mom, Doc Washburn, Family Forward Project advocate and attorney Connie Reguli, and another longtime friend of Hailey's family.

The grief in the room was palpable as, one by one, they testified to the committee about the impact of Rodriguez' crime. It had been four years since he went to prison, but the victims' families still struggled to come to grips with the loss of Hailey and David. A large photo of Hailey stood in front of the podium. The board was handed a photo of Rodriguez' truck with the scooter under it to pass around. Kathy played a video she put together about what happened that day. There was hardly a dry eye among those who came to speak up for those who could no longer speak for themselves.

Kathy anxiously checked the parole board website daily after the hearing, looking for news of the board's verdict. On the morning of August 29, she found the bittersweet news she sought—parole denied, for another two years.

"It's still so hard to believe that we have to keep fighting every two years so far to keep this man behind bars after killing two young adults," she told *Breitbart*. "We don't understand how any state could title him as a 'nonviolent offender' … we relive this horrible crime every time we have to fight his release."[4]

33 - Hear Their Voices

Brooklyn is still not home. Because of the demonstrable fraud in her adoption, Kathy Hall still holds out hope the fraudulent adoption can legally be overturned and Brooklyn can come home to the biological family who love her.

Brooklyn is one of tens of thousands, perhaps hundreds of thousands, of children around the world separated unjustly from their family, whose family cries out for restoration and justice.

Kathy is part of a multitude of parents, grandparents, and relatives who still seek legal avenues to bring their loved ones home. They pray and work every day for laws to change and for their side of the story to be heard. They go to their state capitols and to Washington, D.C., to talk to legislators. Their tears soak the ground as they plead for a miracle.

Others have given up, defeated by a cruel system that ignores their cries. They see no hope of ever seeing their loved ones again. Some turn to drugs and alcohol in their desperation. Others give up entirely on life. To the system, they become a mere statistic, seemingly validating the decision handed down by the court.

There must be a legal mechanism created throughout the United States whereby loving families whose children were taken or adopted out fraudulently can overturn these adoptions and have their children restored to them. In most legal contexts, fraud renders contracts null and void. Foster care and adoption should be no different. In cases where foster care and/or adoption are truly warranted, fraud is unnecessary to make it happen. Any governmental system which relies on fraud and deception in order to exist must be rejected by the taxpayers and citizens.

Family was God's idea. From before the creation of time, God the Father and God the Son existed. God commanded the couple placed in the Garden of Eden to be fruitful and multiply. Children throughout time immemorial are born to a mother and a father. Ancient civilizations measured identity through the family lineage.

Within every child there is an inherent desire to know where he or she came from. The deepest emotional wounds, and the greatest joys, are those related to our families. The severance of such relationships has significant, generational consequences and should never be undertaken lightly.

Real child abuse is a crime and, as such, it should be addressed by the criminal justice system. However, the current system of removing children from one family and giving them to another based on flimsy evidence, petty grounds, or profit is destroying lives and amounts to legalized child trafficking. These families are being ripped apart needlessly. Child Protective Services has become a misnomer, often causing more harm than good for the very children it purports to protect.

There is crossover between CPS and lack of border security. Children come across the border illegally, then some disappear into the foster care system and/or human trafficking. When the child of someone in the country illegally is taken by CPS, these parents may find even fewer resources to reunite their families than parents who are citizens.

Illegal immigration itself takes a huge human toll. Though many who illegally cross our border are otherwise decent people looking for a better life, many others are criminals who come into our country unchecked. When crimes are committed by them, prosecutors and judges too often turn a blind eye. Angel Families grieve, and they cry out for justice for their loved ones. These losses are preventable.

Former Judge Phil Smith's computer is still out there. Linda Collins was brutally murdered days before she was able to reveal its contents publicly, but it still exists. Evidence of children taken by Child Protective Services and used in sex trafficking, child pornography, and pedophilia exists on Smith's computer, including names, places, photos, and money trails. We know where it is—the Arkansas state police have it. Other people have various parts of its contents in their possession.

Some have gone to great lengths to keep this information hidden, but the truth will come out. It always does. The question is: when and by whom? There must be someone with access to the computer's contents who has the courage and integrity to do something about it, or will the computer remain buried in some evidence locker? Will the authorities investigate the computer and its contents to determine what evidence it contains and against whom? Will people go to prison for their crimes against children, or will the perpetrators go the way of Epstein's client list, thinking they got away with it?

The Bible says in Luke 8:17, "For there is nothing hidden that shall not be disclosed, nor anything secret that shall not be known and come out into the open." (AMP) Those people responsible for the crimes in this book and those on Phil Smith's computer will be held accountable one day, whether in this life or the next. That much is certain.

The battle for families is fierce across our nation and even beyond our borders. These are battles we must win.

Hailey King fought valiantly for her baby. David Gutierrez fought courageously for justice. Senator Linda Collins fought till the end for families torn apart by illegal immigration and by Child Protective Services and family courts.

Each of their lives ended before they saw their victories, but through their writings and interviews, and through Kathy Hall's testimony, their voices live on. What they stood for is not over. They now stand with that great cloud of witnesses in the heavenly realm, cheering us on to stand strong and never give up as a new generation picks up their battle cry for justice and freedom. Their voices will not be silenced.

This is not the end.

What happens next is up to people like you.

If you or someone you love is in a battle for your family, I invite you to pray this prayer out loud and make these declarations with me. Add your own declarations. Cut this page out and put it where you see it every day, and pray every day—until you see your breakthrough.

Father God, we want to start out by acknowledging Your goodness and Your love for me and for my family. Even when we can't see it, even when we don't know what is happening, you are still good and You are still working. We say, "Thank You," and we choose to believe that You will somehow work all this out and bring good out of it.

Thank You for the voices of Hailey, David, and Linda, and their inspiration. May their voices never be silenced.

Jesus, You said part of your mission was to set the captives free. You said, "It's not 'four months and then the harvest.' It's NOW." Thank You, God, that You are setting the captives free. It's part of the very reason Jesus came to this planet 2000 years ago. Jesus is unlocking the cages and breaking the chains. Thank You that every trafficker is being exposed and removed. Corruption is being removed in CPS, courts, the legislature, the executive branch, and the alphabet agencies.

Thank You that law enforcement is being cleansed and purified, to go after the real abusers. Lord, we thank you that children are being rescued and restored to loving families.

We thank You, Lord, that every judge, attorney, legislator, social worker, doctor, experimenter, and predator who traffics and enslaves children and families is being brought low in the name of Jesus. They are being removed from their places of authority, and they are being replaced with godly authority.

We recognize that Your heart is always for redemption and salvation. You love the vilest sinner, and You love me. Even now it is not too late for those who have done evil to repent and turn from their wicked ways. Yes, there are consequences, but the blood of Jesus was poured out to save everyone who repents and believes in You. Thank You for saving me despite all my flaws. You are amazing enough to save even those who have hurt my family so much, and I ask You to cause them to have an encounter with You and turn their hearts to You.

We thank You and we declare that Righteousness is being restored in seats of authority in America, and that Justice is being restored in our courts and nation.

We thank You, Lord, for families and children that are being restored, in the mighty name of Yeshua! We pray for healing of every wound in the hearts of the children and for wisdom for every parent trying to help their child heal.

We declare and release Freedom! Lord, we thank You that you are unlocking the freedom of who these children are called to be and the destiny that You have called them to.

Release Chain-Breaker angels to break every chain and set the captives free. Redeem by Your Spirit what the enemy meant for evil. Lord, we say, "Flip the script and turn it to good, for the saving of many lives." In the name of Jesus, amen.

Add your own declarations here:

_____
_____
_____
_____
_____
_____
_____
_____
_____
_____
_____
_____
_____

Voices That Will Not Be Silenced

Appendix 1 ~ God's Heart for Families

Mark 4:22 — For there is nothing hidden which will not be revealed, nor has anything been kept secret but that it should come to light. NKJV

Isaiah 43:5-6 — I am with you now, even close to you, so never yield to fear. I will bring your children from the east; from the west I will gather you. I will say to the north, 'Hand them over!' and to the south, 'Don't hold them back!' Bring me my sons from far away, my daughters from the ends of the earth! TPT

John 8:35 — And slaves have no permanent standing in a family, like a son does, for a son is a part of the family forever. TPT

Mark 10:9 — Therefore what God has joined together, let not man separate. NKJV

Psalm 37:32-34 — Evil ones spy on the godly ones, stalking them to find something they could use to accuse them. They're out for the kill! But God will foil all their plots. The godly will not stand condemned when brought to trial. So don't be impatient for Yahweh to act; keep moving forward steadily in his ways, and he will exalt you to possess the land. You'll watch with your own eyes and see the wicked lose everything. TPT

Isaiah 54:17 — No weapon forged against you will prevail, and you will refute every tongue that accuses you. This is the heritage of the servants of the LORD, and this is their vindication from me," declares the LORD. NIV

Psalm 82:1-2 — All rise! For God now comes to judge as he convenes heaven's courtroom. He judges every judge and rules in the midst of the gods, saying, "How long will you judges refuse to listen to the voice of true justice and continue to corrupt what is right by judging in favor of the wrong?" TPT

Luke 17:2 — It would be better for them to be thrown into the sea with a millstone tied around their neck than to cause one of these little ones to stumble. NIV

I Corinthians 4:5 … He will bring to light what is hidden in darkness and will expose the motives of the heart.… NIV

Romans 8:19 — The entire universe is standing on tiptoe, yearning to see the unveiling of God's glorious sons and daughters! TPT

Matthew 6:10 — Thy kingdom come. Thy will be done in earth, as it is in heaven. KJV

Romans 8:28 — And we know that all things work together for good to them that love God, to them who are the called according to his purpose. KJV

Matthew 10:26 — So do not be afraid of them, for there is nothing concealed that will not be disclosed, or hidden that will not be made known. NIV

Matthew 5:44-45a — However, I [Jesus] say to you, love your enemy, bless the one who curses you, do something wonderful for the one who hates you, and respond to the very ones who persecute you by praying for them. For that will reveal your identity as children of your heavenly Father. TPT

Matthew 21:21-22 — Jesus replied, "Listen to the truth. If you do not doubt God's power and speak out of faith's fullness, you can … say to this mountain, 'Be lifted up and be thrown into the sea,' and it will be done. Everything you pray for with the fullness of faith you will receive. TPT

Hebrews 11:6b — …he who comes to God must believe that He is, and that He is a rewarder of those who diligently seek Him. NKJV

Habakkuk 3:17-18 — Though the fig tree does not blossom and there is no fruit on the vines, though the yield of the olive fails and the fields produce no food, though the flock is cut off from the fold and there are no cattle in the stalls, yet I will [choose to] rejoice in the LORD; I will [choose to] shout in exultation in the [victorious] God of my salvation! AMP

Appendix 1 – God's Heart for Families

Psalm 100:4 — Enter into his gates with thanksgiving, and into his courts with praise: be thankful unto him, and bless his name. KJV

Isaiah 42:3-4 — A bruised reed he will not break, and a smoldering wick he will not snuff out. In faithfulness he will bring forth justice; he will not falter or be discouraged till he establishes justice on earth. In his teaching the islands will put their hope. NIV

Genesis 50:20 — You intended to harm me, but God intended it for good to accomplish what is now being done, the saving of many lives. NIV

Luke 1:37 — For with God nothing shall be impossible. KJV

Philippians 4:13 — I can do all things through Christ who strengthens me. NKJV

Luke 4:18 — "The Spirit of the Lord is upon Me, because He has anointed Me to preach the gospel to the poor; He has sent Me to heal the brokenhearted, to proclaim liberty to the captives and recovery of sight to the blind, to set at liberty those who are oppressed;" NKJV

Luke 18:7-8 — "Don't you know that God, the true judge, will grant justice to all his chosen ones who cry out to Him night and day? He will pour out His Spirit upon them. He will not delay to answer you and give you what you ask for. God will give swift justice to those who don't give up. So be ever praying, ever expecting, in the same way as the widow. Even so, when the Son of Man comes back, will he find this kind of undying faith on earth?" [Jesus] TPT

Psalms 81:10 — I am your only God, the living God. Wasn't I the one who broke the strongholds over you and raised you up out of bondage? Open your mouth with a mighty decree; I will fulfill it now, you'll see! TPT

Proverbs 18:21 — The tongue has the power of life and death, and those who love it will eat its fruit. NIV

Galatians 6:9 — And let us not grow weary while doing good, for in due season we shall reap if we do not lose heart. NKJV

Hebrews 12:1 — Therefore, since we also have such a great cloud of witnesses surrounding us, let's rid ourselves of every obstacle and the sin which so easily entangles us, and let's run with endurance the race that is set before us, NASB

What Scriptures has God spoken to your heart or made alive to you? Write them here. Pray His Word back to Him, and stand in faith on them. He is the Truth, and we can hold on to what He says, no matter what it may look like to our natural eyes.

_____
_____
_____
_____
_____
_____
_____
_____
_____
_____
_____
_____
_____
_____
_____
_____

Appendix 2 ~ Senator Nancy Schaefer on "The Corrupt Business of Child Protective Services"

The late Senator Nancy Schaefer from Georgia wrote a scathing report in 2007 entitled, "The Corrupt Business of Child Protective Services." Like Senator Linda Collins, once she began investigating CPS, she found parents coming out of the woodwork with their heartbreaking stories, backed with evidence, of their children being taken by the state. She also began digging into the agency's dealings and history, and, like Senator Linda Collins, she found disturbing stories she could not ignore.

Her life ended on March 26, 2010. The official story is that her husband killed her in an apparent murder-suicide. There are holes in that explanation, however, and many of her supporters continue to believe her investigation into CPS led to her murder.

Her report released in 2007 certainly led to the loss of her Senate seat. Her courage and tenacity remains an inspiration to advocates and parents today within the Family Rights movement, many of whom meet annually in Washington, D.C., to hold a memorial rally to honor her every year on the anniversary of her death.

She stands with Hailey King, David Gutierrez, and Senator Linda Collins in that "great cloud of witnesses" spoken of in Hebrews 12, cheering us on as we pray and fight for God's heart for families.

Following is the text of her ground-breaking report.

From the legislative desk of Senator Nancy Schaefer[1]

November 16, 2007

Updated: September 25, 2008

The Corrupt Business of Child Protective Services

By: Nancy Schaefer

Senator, 50th District Georgia

My introduction into child protective service cases was due to a grandmother in an adjoining state who called me with her tragic story. Her two granddaughters had been taken from her daughter who lived in my district. Her daughter was told wrongly that if she wanted to see her children again she should sign a paper and give up her children. Frightened and young, the daughter did. I have since discovered that parents are often threatened into cooperation of permanent separation of their children.

The children were taken to another county and placed in foster care. The foster parents were told wrongly that they could adopt the children. The grandmother then jumped through every hoop known to man in order to get her granddaughters. When the case finally came to court it was made evident by one of the foster parent's children that the foster parents had, at any given time, 18 foster children and that the foster mother had an inappropriate relationship with the caseworker.

In the courtroom, the juvenile judge, acted as though she was shocked and said the two girls would be removed quickly. They were not removed. Finally, after much pressure being applied to the Department of Family and Children Services of Georgia (DFCS), the children were driven to South Georgia to meet their grandmother who gladly drove to meet them. After being with their grandmother two or three days, the judge, quite out of the blue, wrote up a new order to send the girls to their father, who previously had no interest in the case and who lived on the West Coast. The father was in "adult entertainment". His girlfriend worked as an "escort" and his brother, who also worked in the business, had a sexual charge brought against him.

Within a couple of days the father was knocking on the grandmother's door and took the girls kicking and screaming to California.

The father developed an unusual relationship with the former foster parents and soon moved back to the southeast, and the foster parents began driving to the father's residence and picking up the little girls for visits. The oldest child had told her mother and grandmother on two different occasions that the foster father molested her.

To this day after five years, this loving, caring blood relative grandmother does not even have visitation privileges with the children. The little girls are in my opinion permanently traumatized and the young mother of the girls was so traumatized with shock when the girls were first removed from her that she has not recovered.

Throughout this case and through the process of dealing with multiple other mismanaged cases of the Department of Family and Children Services (DFCS), I have worked with other desperate parents and children across the state because they have no rights and no one with whom to turn. I have witnessed ruthless behavior from many caseworkers, social workers, investigators, lawyers, judges, therapists, and others such as those who "pick up" the children. I have been stunned by what I have seen and heard from victims all over the state of Georgia.

In this report, I am focusing on the Georgia Department of Family and Children Services (DFCS). However, I believe Child Protective Services nationwide has become corrupt and that the entire system is broken almost beyond repair. I am convinced parents and families should be warned of the dangers.

The Department of Child Protective Services, known as the Department of Family and Children Service (DFCS) in Georgia and other titles in other states, has become a "protected empire" built on taking children and separating families. This is not to say that there are not those children who do need to be removed from wretched situations and need protection. This report is concerned with the children and parents caught up in "legal kidnapping," ineffective policies, and DFCS who do does not remove a child or children when a child is enduring torment and abuse. (See Exhibit A and Exhibit B)

In one county in my District, I arranged a meeting for thirty-seven families to speak freely and without fear. These poor parents and grandparents spoke of their painful, heart wrenching encounters with DFCS. Their suffering was overwhelming. They wept and cried. Some did not know where their children were and had not seen them in years. I had witnessed the "Gestapo" at work and I witnessed the deceitful conditions under which children were taken in the middle of the night, out of hospitals, off of school buses, and out of homes. In one county a private drug testing business was operating within the DFCS department that required many, many drug tests from parents and individuals for profit. In another county children were not removed when they were enduring the worst possible abuse. Due to being exposed, several employees in a particular DFCS office were fired. However, they have now been rehired either in neighboring counties or in the same county again. According to the calls I am now receiving, the conditions in that county are returning to the same practices that they had before the light was shown on their deeds. Having worked with probably 300 cases statewide, I am convinced there is no responsibility and no accountability in the system.

I have come to the conclusion:

- that poor parents often times are targeted to lose their children because they do not have the where-with-all to hire lawyers and fight the system. Being poor does not mean you are not a good parent or that you do not love your child, or that your child should be removed and placed with strangers;

- that all parents are capable of making mistakes and that making a mistake does not mean your children are always to be removed from the home. Even if the

Appendix 2 – Senator Nancy Schaefer

home is not perfect, it is home; and that's where a child is the safest and where he or she wants to be, with family;

- that parenting classes, anger management classes, counseling referrals, therapy classes and on and on are demanded of parents with no compassion by the system even while they are at work and while their children are separated from them. This can take months or even years and it emotionally devastates both children and parents. Parents are victimized by "the system" that makes a profit for holding children longer and "bonuses" for not returning children;

- that caseworkers and social workers are oftentimes guilty of fraud. They withhold evidence. They fabricate evidence and they seek to terminate parental rights. However, when charges are made against them, the charges are ignored;

- that the separation of families is growing as a business because local governments have grown accustomed to having taxpayer dollars to balance their ever-expanding budgets;

- that Child Protective Service and Juvenile Court can always hide behind a confidentiality clause in order to protect their decisions and keep the funds flowing. There should be open records and "court watches"! Look who is being paid! There are state employees, lawyers, court investigators, court personnel, and judges. There are psychologists, and psychiatrists, counselors, caseworkers, therapists, foster parents, adoptive parents, and on and on. All are looking to the children in state custody to provide job security. Parents do not realize that social workers are the glue that holds "the system" together that funds the court, the child's attorney, and the multiple other jobs including DFCS's attorney.

- that The Adoption and the Safe Families Act, set in motion by President Bill Clinton, offered cash "bonuses" to the states for every child they adopted out of foster care. In order to receive the "adoption incentive bonuses" local child protective services need more children. They must have merchandise (children) that sell and you must have plenty of them so the buyer can choose. Some counties are known to give a $4,000 bonus for each child adopted and an additional $2,000 for a "special needs" child. Employees work to keep the federal dollars flowing;

- that there is double dipping. The funding continues as long as the child is out of the home. When a child in foster care is placed with a new family then "adoption bonus funds" are available. When a child is placed in a mental health facility and is on 16 drugs per day, like two children of a constituent of mine, more funds are involved;

- that there are no financial resources and no real drive to unite a family and help keep them together;

- that the incentive for social workers to return children to their parents quickly after taking them has disappeared and who in protective services will step up to the plate and say, "This must end!" No one, because they are all in the system together and a system with no leader and no clear policies will always fail the children. Look at the waste in government that is forced upon the tax payer;

- that the "Policy Manuel" is considered "the last word" for DFCS. However, it is too long, too confusing, poorly written and does not take the law into consideration;

- that if the lives of children were improved by removing them from their homes, there might be a greater need for protective services, but today all children are not always safer. Children, of whom I am aware, have been raped and impregnated in foster care and the head of a Foster Parents Association in my District was recently arrested because of child molestation;

- that some parents are even told if they want to see their children or grandchildren, they must divorce their spouse. Many, who are under privileged, feeling they have no option, will divorce and then just continue to live together. This is an anti-family policy, but parents will do anything to get their children home with them.

- fathers, (non-custodial parents) I must add, are oftentimes treated as criminals without access to their own children and have child support payments strangling the very life out of them;

- that the Foster Parents Bill of Rights does not bring out that a foster parent is there only to care for a child until the child can be returned home. Many Foster Parents today use the Foster Parent Bill of Rights to hire a lawyer and seek to adopt the child from the real parents, who are desperately trying to get their child home and out of the system;

- that tax dollars are being used to keep this gigantic system afloat, yet the victims, parents, grandparents, guardians and especially the children, are charged for the system's services.

- that grandparents have called from all over the State of Georgia trying to get custody of their grandchildren. DFCS claims relatives are contacted, but there are cases that prove differently. Grandparents who lose their grandchildren to strangers have lost their own flesh and blood. The children lose their family heritage and grandparents, and parents too, lose all connections to their heirs.

- that The National Center on Child Abuse and Neglect in 1998 reported that six times as many children died in foster care than in the general public and that once removed to official "safety", these children are far more likely to suffer abuse, including sexual molestation than in the general population.

- that according to the California Little Hoover Commission Report in 2003, 30% to 70% of the children in California group homes do not belong there and should not have been removed from their homes.

FINAL REMARKS

On my desk are scores of cases of exhausted families and troubled children. It has been beyond me to turn my back on these suffering, crying, and sometimes beaten down individuals. We are mistreating the most innocent. Child Protective Services have become adult centered to the detriment of children. No longer is judgment based on what the child needs or who the child wants to be with or what is really best for the whole family; it is some adult or bureaucrat who makes the decisions, based often on just hearsay, without ever consulting a family member, or just what is convenient, profitable, or less troublesome for a director of DFCS.

I have witnessed such injustice and harm brought to these families that I am not sure if I even believe reform of the system is possible! The system cannot be trusted. It does not serve the people. It obliterates families and children simply because it has the power to do so. Children deserve better. Families deserve better. It's time to pull back the curtain and set our children and families free.

"Speak up for those who cannot speak for themselves, for the rights of all who are destitute. Speak up and judge fairly; defend the rights of the poor and the needy." Proverbs 31:8-9

RECOMMENDATIONS

1. Call for an independent audit of the Department of Family and Children's Services (DFCS) to expose corruption and fraud.

2. Activate immediate change. Every day that passes means more families and children are subject to being held hostage.

3. End the financial incentives that separate families.

4. Grant to parents their rights in writing.

5. Mandate a search for family members to be given the opportunity to adopt their own relatives.

6. Mandate a jury trial where every piece of evidence is presented before removing a child from his or her parents.

7. Require a warrant or a positive emergency circumstance before removing children from their parents. (Judge Arthur G. Christean, Utah Bar Journal, January, 1997 reported that "except in emergency circumstances, including the need for immediate medical care, require warrants upon affidavits of probable cause before entry upon private property is permitted for the forcible removal of children from their parents.")

8. Uphold the laws when someone fabricates or presents false evidence. If a parent alleges fraud, hold a hearing with the right to discovery of all evidence.

Appendix 3 ~ Guardianship Abuse

It is not just children who are being ripped from loving families in America. The elderly and disabled adults are also vulnerable to unscrupulous removals from their families through fraudulent guardianships, Adult Protective Services, and corrupt players within the probate court system.

Through my years of investigative research with MedicalKidnap.com and RealNewsSpark.com, I found that probate courts in America are subject to the many of the same kinds of problems seen in family courts and juvenile courts. There is frequently a lack of due process. Bad actors abound in the legal, medical, and judicial fields where senior citizens are involved.

At stake are the lives, freedom, health, and estates of thousands of elderly and disabled Americans. There are at least three times as many people under guardianship than children in foster care, to the tune of billions of dollars a year. With the stroke of a probate judge's pen, a senior citizen can lose every freedom they had as a citizen of the United States and as a human being. They lose the ability to have a voice in their own care.

Guardianship laws were historically put in place to protect and provide for people who have lost the cognitive or physical ability to care for themselves. People in a coma or who suffer from dementia must have people in place to help them. However, such humanitarian laws and provisions are now being exploited and used to seize the property, estates, and freedoms of people who are not incapacitated.

All it takes is for one compromised doctor, lawyer, or social worker to state a person is incapacitated, even if the statement is false, and a judge can sign off on it and assign a court-appointed guardian. Suddenly the victim loses everything without ever showing up in a courtroom. Sometimes, they are completely unaware that a court hearing even happened.

Judges can and do set aside documents of medical powers of attorney or other such documents the senior citizen painstakingly prepared in advance to protect themselves. Through guardianship and conservatorship, a guardian who may never have met their new ward, who may have no interest in the person's well-being or wishes, now controls their life.

Lonnie Brennan, editor of the *Boston Broadside*, describes the process as "Isolate, Medicate, Liquidate."[1] The guardian can forbid the victim's loved ones to have any visits or contact. They may remove the person from their home and put them in a nursing home without their consent. They can approve or deny medications or medical courses of treatment regardless of the ward's wishes. The ward may be drugged into oblivion against their will. The guardian can sell their house, property, and all their belongings, while the guardian pockets large portions of the financial proceeds.

The victims of these legalized criminal enterprises range from wealthy and prominent citizens to the poorest among us, and there is little to no oversight or accountability for the whole process.

Heartbreaking stories include that of Joann Bashinsky, beloved Alabama philanthropist and Golden Flake heiress, forced into guardianship with a court-appointed guardian by the decree of a judge over false allegations that she suffered from dementia.[2]

Retired schoolteacher Marian Leonard was isolated from her family and forced into hospice care, though she had no terminal illness. She was simply old—and had an estate of 300 acres of prime timber land.[3]

Marvin Seigel's estate of about $9 million was milked down to a million dollars by the time he passed away. His loving daughter and her family were kicked out of his home just before Christmas when guardians seized control of his life.[4]

Others with little money or assets are taken into guardianship, forced into nursing homes, and medicated until the limits of their Medicare benefits are reached. Then, they are quietly given medications which hasten their death.

Just as with the Child Protective and foster care/adoption system, exposure, investigation, and a complete overhaul needs to take place of the guardianship system so that families with old and young alike are no longer ripped apart by bureaucrats who profit financially from the destruction of families and the trafficking of other human beings.

Acknowledgements

My heart is full of gratitude, first, to the Lord Jesus who has held me and equipped me throughout every step of this book.

I have always had a passion for truth and justice. It was the owner/editor of *Health Impact News* who gave me the opportunity and platform to investigate stories for MedicalKidnap.com. Thank you, Brian Shilhavy, and the MK team for inviting me into this arena. It completely changed my life.

Carla Hartley, my late mentor and friend, founder of Ancient Art Midwifery Institute, thank you for the many deep conversations and your support. I was on track to finish the school and become a full-fledged midwife. I loved attending births and teaching about childbirth, breastfeeding, and bonding. When I agonized over the question, "What good does it do to have a great birth if the state is just going to come in and take your baby?" you gave me your blessing and the wings to lay down all my midwifery plans and launch fully into investigating medical kidnapping stories. You said, "This is a battle we MUST win."

The season at MedicalKidnap.com both opened my eyes and overwhelmed me, and I had to step away at the end of 2018 to regroup. To the leadership of Family Forward Project, especially Kathleen Arthur and Connie Reguli, thank you for bringing me into your vital advocacy work for families. Thank you for believing in me and encouraging me to remain engaged even when I was tempted to lose hope.

To the faculty and students of King's Way College, any words of thanks I can muster fall far short of the depth of my gratitude for you. Pastors Jason Hooper and

Tim Beck, God used you to transform me from someone who wanted to help but didn't know how, into an overcomer, equipped to do whatever God calls me to do. Thank you for giving God your "Yes" and always pushing us to go deeper. Pastor Adam Pruitt, your riveting historic storytelling has infused me with courage to continue this journey, no matter the cost. Joshua and Janet Mills, Dr. Brian Simmons, Roberts Liardon, Tina Hooper, and Sarah Wright, along with Pastors Tim and Jason, thank you for not only teaching, but imparting incredible wisdom from the throne of heaven.

To the worship team, including Jeff and Suz Whatley, Joshua Mills, and Jonathan Newman, thank you for faithfully shifting the atmosphere and bringing us into a place of intimacy and encounter with the King of Glory. So much of this book was written under the anointing of this incredible worship. Christina, Ellen, Sue, Hope, Holly, Laurie, James and Renee, Noreen, Debbie, Judith, Donna, Claudia, and many more—thanks so much for your prayers, words of wisdom, and encouragement to stay the course and get to the finish line.

To Kyle, Gene, and Mandy of Jumpmaster Press, thank you for allowing me to be a part of your incredible writing seminars. Though your niche is sci-fi and fantasy, not non-fiction, I have learned much about the art of writing from you. Thank you for all your encouragement and wisdom.

Finally, to my wonderful (and patient) family, thank you for loving me and putting up with me through this seemingly endless process. There have been so many times I couldn't get away or go out because I was "working on the book." I know, my sweet husband, you had to wonder if I was ever going to finish this book! Thank you for cooking or bringing home supper when I was too "in the zone" to cook, and for all the countless ways you love me so well. You are the best! "Frodo wouldn't have gotten far without Sam."

About the Author

Terri LaPoint is, above all else, passionately in love with Jesus, devoted to truth and freedom. She is a wife, mother, and writer. After years of being a homeschool mom, breastfeeding educator, labor doula, and assistant midwife, she brought her love of family and understanding of the bond between parents and children into research and writing.

For several years she was the lead investigative journalist and assistant editor for MedicalKidnap.com, a division of *Health Impact News*, where she investigated and wrote articles on hundreds of cases involving people taken from their families by Child Protective Services, Adult Protective Services, and guardianships. She simply wanted to find the truth of what was happening to families all over America. The facts and the data of her investigations caused her to recognize there is a serious threat to families everywhere. She could not un-see what she had seen, but she knew that God's heart is for families, restoration, and redemption.

She is a contributing author to several books, including *Medical Kidnapping: A Threat to Every Family in America*, *PolitiChicks: A Clarion Call to Political Activism,* and *The New Child Abuse Pediatrician: Doctors become Prosecutors*. Her articles have appeared in *PolitiChicks*, *PPJ Gazette*, the *Inquisitr*, *The Liberty Beacon*, and *Midwifery Today*. Terri is a regular guest on blogtalk radio programs and speaks to family rights groups. She has been a guest on *America Trends* with Dr. Gina Loudon, and was featured in a documentary on Medical Kidnapping by *Michelle Malkin Investigates*. In 2017 she received Michelle Malkin's Bulldog Award for her tenacious work on medical kidnapping.

She holds a B.S. in Cultural Anthropology/World Missions from Toccoa Falls

College. She studied midwifery through Ancient Art Midwifery Institute, and she recently graduated from King's Way College–a unique ministry school that trains people to transform culture and make a difference in their sphere of influence.

Terri LaPoint's work continues as she speaks, writes, educates lawmakers and the public, and advocates for change. See her website and some of her articles at RealNewsSpark.com and follow her on Facebook. For speaking engagements, email her at Voices.RealNewsSpark@proton.me

Citations and End Notes

Chapter 1 – Different from the Others
[1] Name has been changed.

Chapter 2 – A Knock on the Door
[1] Kathy Hall, "Victim Impact Statement" at Sergio Rodriguez's sentencing hearing, April 11, 2018.
[2] "We Hold These Truths, Live with Kathy Hall" blogtalk show hosted by Seraphim Schwab, *The Family Rights Movement,* August 29, 2019. www.youtube.com/watch?v=xACS2W8oyls&t=18s

Chapter 4 – It's Not Supposed to Work This Way
[1] Ibid.

Chapter 5 – Downward Spiral
[1] Ibid.

Chapter 6 – Sirens, and More Sirens
[1] Name has been changed.
[2] Name has been changed.

Chapter 7 - Hailey
[1] Name has been changed.

Chapter 8 - David
[1] "What Happened to Linda Collins, AR St. Senator? Kathryn Hall & David Gutierrez share some insight." *Debbie Aldrich Show,* June 9, 2019. www.youtube.com/watch?v=q9gU1Qjkwto&t=3937s

Chapter 9 – Fighting for Justice

[1] For a good description of ASFA and its impact, read "In defense of parents in the child welfare system," by attorney Connie Reguli, *Child Welfare and Family Law and Reform*, 8/14/2016.
https://tennfamilylaw.wordpress.com/2016/08/14/in-defense-of-parents-in-the-child-welfare-system/

[2] "Illegal Alien Manslaughter in AR: Katherine Hall, Linda Collins & David Gutierrez Tell Their Story," Interview by Paul Harrell, *Conduit News*, May 16, 2019. www.youtube.com/watch?v=ex0AFnY9dTc&t=5s

Chapter 10 – Where Is Justice?

[1] "Angel Mom, Kathy Hall Joins Me Live," hosted by Jim White, *Northwest Liberty News*, December 17, 2019.
www.facebook.com/northwestlibertynews/videos/462683627768701

Chapter 13 – "You Have Help Now"

[1] "Unlicensed to Kill," Federation for American Immigration Reform, September 2006.
www.fairus.org/issue/illegal-immigration/unlicensed-kill Accessed 8/26/2021

[2] "Rep. Linda Collins-Smith announces she is switching from Democrat to Republican," YouTube video, Jason Tolbert, August 10, 2011.
www.youtube.com/watch?v=RtvPv_0aly0

[3] "Collins-Smith announces State Senate Candidacy," Tammy Curtis, *Areawide Media*, November 26, 2011. www.areawidenews.com/story/1788365.html Accessed 10/17/2021

[4] "Linda Collins Smith asks and talks about Faith Based Partners & Healthcare for Foster Children !" hosted by Paul Harrell, *Conduit Media Group*, December 31, 2016.
www.youtube.com/watch?v=7UmvaiYi6bY&t=9s

[5] "7 Children Kidnapped by State of Arkansas from Homeschool Family to Remain in State Custody," Terri LaPoint, *Medical Kidnap*, February 16, 2015.
https://medicalkidnap.com/2015/02/16/7-children-kidnapped-by-state-of-arkansas-from-homeschool-family-to-remain-in-state-custody/

[6] "Arkansas Senator Writes to DHS "The Gloves are About to Come Off" as Cover-up in Stanley Case is Discovered," *Health Impact News* editor, *Medical Kidnap*, October 17, 2016

https://medicalkidnap.com/2016/10/17/arkansas-senator-writes-to-dhs-the-gloves-are-about-to-come-off-as-cover-up-in-stanley-case-is-discovered/

[7] Facebook post by Alan Clark, February 10, 2022.

[8] "Clark says DHS email proves 'cover-up'," David Showers, *The Sentinel-Record*, October 13, 2016. www.hotsr.com/news/2016/oct/13/clark-says-dhs-email-proves-cover-up-20/

Chapter 14 - Secrets

[1] "The AFCARS Report, 2022," U.S. Department of Health and Human Services, Administration for Children and Families, Administration on Children, Youth and Families, Children's Bureau. www.acf.hhs.gov/sites/default/files/documents/cb/afcars-report-29.pdf

[2] "Child Maltreatment 2021," U.S. Department of Health and Human Services, Administration for Children and Families, Administration on Children, Youth and Families, Children's Bureau, February 9, 2023. www.acf.hhs.gov/cb/report/child-maltreatment-2021

[3] "Judges Reject Claim That Social Workers Didn't Know Lying In Court to Remove Children Was Wrong," R. Scott Moxley, *OC Weekly*, January 6, 2017.

www.ocweekly.com/judges-reject-orange-countys-claim-that-social-workers-didnt-know-lying-in-court-was-wrong-7774616/

See video of the exchange between attorneys for the social workers and the panel of judges - "15-55563 Preslie Hardwick v. Marcia Vreeken," *United States Court of Appeals for the Ninth Circuit*, October 7, 2016. https://www.youtube.com/watch?v=nZa0LxmFTkI

[4] "Republican Lawmakers Block Townsend Amendments To Protect Parents From Dishonest DCS Workers," Loretta Hunnicut, *Arizona Daily Independent News Network*, April 18, 2017.
https://arizonadailyindependent.com/2017/04/18/republican-lawmakers-block-townsend-amendment-to-protect-parents-from-dishonest-dcs-workers/ Accessed 10/23/2021

Chapter 15 – Never Forgotten

[1] 'Angel Families', Trump aides rally against illegal immigrant crime," Alex Pappas, *Fox News*, September 7, 2018. www.foxnews.com/politics/angel-families-trump-aides-rally-against-illegal-immigrant-crime Accessed 10/29/2021

Chapter 16 – Little Rock

[1] www.facebook.com/reggie.cowan.1/videos/2091105500929228

[2] "Arkansas Senator Issues "Child Welfare Manifesto" – Child Abuse Perpetrated by the State Must Stop," *Medical Kidnap* staff, *Medical Kidnap*. January 3, 2017. https://medicalkidnap.com/2017/01/03/arkansas-senator-issues-child-welfare-manifesto-child-abuse-perpetrated-by-the-state-must-stop/

[3] For a good description of ASFA and its impact, read "In defense of parents in the child welfare system," by attorney Connie Reguli, 8/14/2016. https://tennfamilylaw.wordpress.com/2016/08/14/in-defense-of-parents-in-the-child-welfare-system/

[4] "RIGHT NOW Interview: Arkansas State Senator Linda Collins-Smith," Interview by Mary Freeman, March 26, 2019.
https://newrightnetwork.com/2019/03/right-now-interview-arkansas-state-senator-linda-collins-smith.html Accessed 3/19/2020

[5] "Angel Mom, Kathy Hall Joins Me Live," hosted by Jim White, *Northwest Liberty News*, December 17, 2019.
www.facebook.com/northwestlibertynews/videos/462683627768701

Chapter 17 – Family Forward Project

[1] Divorce appeal document - https://237995-729345-1-raikfcquaxqncofqfm.stackpathdns.com/wp-content/uploads/2019/06/collinsappeal.pdf

[2] https://www.facebook.com/kenneth.wallis.7/videos/10101121629019456

Chapter 19 – She Had it All Along

[1] "Watch Live: Angel Families and Women for Trump Rally for Border Security on Capitol Hill," Michelle Moons, *Breitbart*, January 15, 2019. Kathy Hall tells Hailey's story beginning at the one hour mark on the video.
www.breitbart.com/politics/2019/01/15/watch-live-angel-families-and-women-for-trump-rally-for-border-security-on-capitol-hill/

[2] Women for America First, *Facebook*, January 15, 2019.
www.facebook.com/WomenForAmericaFirst/videos/401523403943558/

[3] "Nancy Pelosi Refuses to Meet with Angel Moms Protesting Inside Her Office," Joshua Caplain, *Breitbart*, January 15, 2019.

www.breitbart.com/politics/2019/01/15/nancy-pelosi-refuses-to-meet-with-angel-moms-protesting-inside-her-office/

[4] "Sean Hannity: Pelosi is too busy hating Trump to care about shutdowns, furloughed workers and angel moms," Sean Hannity, *Fox News*, January 18, 2019. www.foxnews.com/opinion/sean-hannity-pelosi-is-too-busy-hating-trump-to-care-about-shutdowns-furloughed-workers-and-angel-moms

[5] "Angel Moms Storm Chuck Schumer's Office: 'Get the Wall Done, Randy DeSoto, *Western Journal*, January 15, 2019. www.westernjournal.com/angel-moms-storm-chuck-schumers-office-get-wall-done/

Chapter 20 – Angel Families

[1] "Watch Live: Angel Families, America First Group Hold 'Secure the Border' Rally on Capitol Hill," Michelle Moons, *Breitbart*. February 13, 2019. www.breitbart.com/politics/2019/02/13/angel-families-and-america-first-group-hold-secure-the-border-rally-on-capitol-hill/

[2] "Angel families, 'Women for Trump' rally with GOP lawmakers for border wall," *One America News Network (OAN)*, February 14, 2019. www.youtube.com/watch?v=qR8VcV111sc

[3] "Family of teacher killed, learns suspect had criminal past and was in US illegally," Genevieve Curtis, *KFOX14*, November 24, 2018. https://kfoxtv.com/news/local/family-of-teacher-killed-learns-suspect-had-criminal-past-and-in-us-illegally

[4] "Angel Mom Michelle Root Who Lost Her Daughter to Illegal Immigrant Says, 'Angel Families Are the End Result of Open Borders, Julie Carr, *Tennessee Star*, September 6, 2019. https://tennesseestar.com/2019/09/06/angel-mom-michelle-root-who-lost-her-daughter-to-illegal-immigrant-says-angel-families-are-the-end-result-of-open-borders/

[5] U.S. Customs and Border Protection website, In Memoriam, Javier Vega, Jr. https://www.cbp.gov/about/in-memoriam/javier-vega-jr

[6] "Watch–Mo Brooks: Democrats 'Aiding and Abetting' 2K Illegal Alien Killings Every Year," John Binder, *Breitbart*, January 15, 2019. www.breitbart.com/politics/2019/01/15/watch-mo-brooks-democrats-aiding-and-abetting-2k-illegal-alien-killings-every-year/

[7] "RIGHT NOW Interview: Arkansas State Senator Linda Collins-Smith," Mary Freeman, *New Right Network*, March 26, 2019.

https://newrightnetwork.com/2019/03/right-now-interview-arkansas-state-senator-linda-collins-smith.html

Chapter 21 – Adventures in DC
[1] Name has been changed.

Chapter 22 – No Slowing Down
[1] https://www.facebook.com/angelmomkh/videos/2316188258662713
[2] "Judicial Watch: FBI Admits Hillary Clinton Emails Found in Obama White House," *Judicial Watch*, April 23, 2019. www.judicialwatch.org/judicial-watch-fbi-admits-hillary-clinton-emails-found-in-obama-white-house/
[3] "Angel Moms Remember Their Children on Mother's Day: 'The Hurt and Pain Will Never Go Away, John Binder, *Breitbart*, May 12, 2019. www.breitbart.com/politics/2019/05/12/angel-moms-remember-children-mothers-day-hurt-pain-will-never-go-away/
[4] Not his real name

Chapter 24 – A Right Way and a Wrong Way
[1] "Illegal Alien Manslaughter in AR: Katherine Hall, Linda Collins & David Gutierrez Tell Their Story," hosted by Paul Harrell, *Conduit News Radio*, May 16, 2019. www.youtube.com/watch?v=ex0AFnY9dTc&t=26s
[2] Ibid.

Chapter 25 - Followed
[1] "Chris Cox (NRA), Senators Linda Collins-Smith, and Trent Garner re: 2nd Amendment in Arkansas," *Doc Washburn Show*, KARN FM Radio, March 29, 2017.

Chapter 27 – Something's Wrong
[1] "Iowa DHS social worker charged with lying in child removal case," *WQAD Digital Team,* April 11, 2019. www.wqad.com/article/news/crime/iowa-dhs-social-worker-charged-with-lying-in-child-removal-case/526-a9415a23-b15c-4399-871b-f397798ece9e
[2] "Police: Lab owner falsified drug screen test results to Dale County DHR," Michele Forehand, *Dothan Eagle*, May 10, 2019.

https://dothaneagle.com/news/crime_court/police-lab-owner-falsified-drug-screen-test-results-to-dale-county-dhr/article_0204a086-7342-11e9-a4dd-879fec3b6fb0.html Accessed 2/19/2022.

3 Name has been changed.

4 "Kathy Hall Interview on Linda Collins-Smith's Murder," *Doc Washburn Show*, *KARN FM*, August 19, 2020.

Chapter 28 – Kill Switch

1 "Former Arkansas State Senator's Death Being Investigated As Homicide," Julianna Clipson, *5 News KFSM*, June 5, 2019. www.5newsonline.com/article/news/local/outreach/back-to-school/former-arkansas-state-senators-death-being-investigated-as-homicide/ Accessed 3/9/2020.

2 "Ken Yang Reacts to Death of Linda Collins," hosted by Paul Harrell, *Conduit News Radio*, June 5, 2019. www.youtube.com/watch?v=rljmN6Mk6BA&t=464s Accessed 2/21/2022.

3 Ibid.

4 "Judge to finally unseal documents in murder of former state Sen. Linda Collins-Smith," Kate Holland and Josh Margolin, *ABC News*, June 12, 2020. https://abcnews.go.com/US/judge-finally-unseal-documents-murder-state-sen-linda/story?id=71228614

5 "New documents released in O'Donnell murder case show motive in Linda Collins murder," Region 8 Newsdesk, *KAIT*, August 22, 2020. www.kait8.com/2020/08/21/new-documents-released-odonnell-murder-case/ Accessed 10/27/2021

6 Max Brantley, senior editor of the *Arkansas Times*, is the husband of the judge in the Smiths' contentious divorce case, Ellen Brantley. Over the years, Max Brantley has written several negative pieces on Senator Linda Collins-Smith—a point some, including Doc Washburn of KARN FM radio, have found problematic.
"Doc Roasts Max Brantley Over Linda Collins-Smith Murder Arrest Story, Vol. 1," *Doc Washburn Show*, June 18, 2019.

Chapter 29 – We Got You

1 "Family reacts to loss days after former Arkansas senator found dead outside home," Michael R. Wickline, *Arkansas Democrat-Gazette*, June 12, 2019.

www.arkansasonline.com/news/2019/jun/12/ex-senator-s-family-reacts-to-loss-2019/

[2] "Former Arkansas State Senator's Death Being Investigated As Homicide," Julianna Clipson, *KFSM 5 News*, June 5, 2019. www.5newsonline.com/article/news/local/outreach/back-to-school/former-arkansas-state-senators-death-being-investigated-as-homicide/527-81e20ab3-ed26-4953-8b73-59b1330c1798

[3] Ibid.

[4] "Woman arrested in connection to killing of former Arkansas state Sen. Linda Collins-Smith," Anthony Rivas, *ABC News*, June 15, 2019. https://abcnews.go.com/US/woman-arrested-connection-killing-arkansas-state-senator-linda/story?id=63727329

[5] "Family reacts to loss days after former Arkansas senator found dead outside home," Michael R. Wickline, *Arkansas Democrat-Gazette*, June 12, 2019. www.arkansasonline.com/news/2019/jun/12/ex-senator-s-family-reacts-to-loss-2019/

[6] "Conduit News Radio with Paul Harrell - 6/14/19," *Conduit News*, June 14, 2019. www.youtube.com/watch?v=A8BGFGTwuf8&t=3333s

[7] "The Hands of a Killer," *Dateline NBC*, April 8, 2022. www.nbcnews.com/dateline/watch-dateline-episode-hands-killer-now-n1294322

[8] "Video shows woman put knife in purse moments after Arkansas ex-legislator was stabbed to death," *KARK Little Rock*, December 15, 2021. https://news.yahoo.com/video-shows-woman-put-knife-162900392.html Accessed 12/21/2021

[9] "The Hands of a Killer," *Dateline NBC*, April 8, 2022.

[10] "Feds admit reason for computer wipe in Woods kickback case not credible," Doug Thompson, *Northwest Arkansas Democrat Gazette*, February 16, 2018.
www.nwaonline.com/news/2018/feb/16/all-recordings-found-in-woods-corruptio/

Chapter 31 – Trafficking and Fraud

[1] "We Hold These Truths, Live with Kathy Hall" show with Seraphim Schwab, *The Family Rights Movement,* August 29, 2019. www.youtube.com/watch?v=xACS2W8oyls&t=18s

[2] "Navy Dad Goes on Hunger Strike in Kansas Until State-Kidnapped Children are Returned or He Starves to Death," *Medical Kidnap* staff [Terri LaPoint], *Medical Kidnap*, March 19, 2016.
https://medicalkidnap.com/2016/03/19/navy-dad-goes-on-hunger-strike-in-kansas-until-state-kidnapped-children-are-returned-or-he-starves-to-death/

[3] "Mother's Day Reunion: Military Dad and Mom Reunited with Children 3 Years After Kansas Took Them Over Medical Cannabis," *Medical Kidnap* staff [Terri LaPoint], *Medical Kidnap*, May 11, 2018.
https://medicalkidnap.com/2018/05/11/mothers-day-reunion-military-dad-and-mom-reunited-with-children-3-years-after-kansas-took-them-over-medical-cannabis/

[4] "The Medical Kidnap Show - Episode 6," hosted by Brian Shilhavy, *Medical Kidnap*, November 10, 2019. www.youtube.com/watch?v=0Ccx18RJI0o

[5] "Arizona Adoption Attorney Arrested For Adoption Fraud And Alien Smuggling," *United States Department of Justice*, October 9, 2019. www.justice.gov/usao-wdar/pr/arizona-adoption-attorney-arrested-adoption-fraud-and-alien-smuggling

[6] "Marshallese Adoptions Fuel A Lucrative Practice For Some Lawyers," John Hill and Emily Dugdale, *Honolulu Civil Beat*, November 28, 2018. www.civilbeat.org/2018/11/marshallese-adoptions-fuel-a-lucrative-practice-for-some-lawyers/

[7] "Angel Mom, Kathy Hall Joins Me Live," hosted by Jim White, *Northwest Liberty News*, December 17, 2019.
www.facebook.com/northwestlibertynews/videos/462683627768701

Chapter 32 – Twists and Turns, and an Explosion

[1] "NEW DETAILS: Rebecca O'Donnell, a bloody knife and a chicken," Region 8 Newsdesk, *KAIT 8*, August 14, 2020.
www.kait8.com/2020/08/14/new-details-rebecca-odonnell-bloody-knife-chicken/

[2] "In bombshell plea, close friend admits to murdering former Arkansas state senator," Tammy Glass, Chris Francescani, and Kate Holland, *ABC News*, August 6, 2020. https://abcnews.go.com/US/bombshell-plea-close-friend-admits-murdering-arkansas-state/story?id=72214576

[3] Ibid.

[4] "Angel Mom Celebrates as Daughter's Illegal Alien Killer Is Denied Parole: 'Thank the Lord," John Binder, *Breitbart*, August 30, 2022.

www.breitbart.com/politics/2022/08/30/angel-mom-celebrates-as-daughters-illegal-alien-killer-is-denied-parole-thank-the-lord/

Appendix 2 ~ Senator Nancy Schaefer on "The Corrupt Business of Child Protective Services"

[1] https://parentalrights.org/wp-content/uploads/2017/05/CBCP.pdf

Appendix 3 ~ Guardianship Abuse

[1] "Isolate, Medicate, Liquidate: How to Fleece a Senior - Warning to Seniors: Rich or Poor, You're Worth a LOT to Lawyers, Courts, and Service Agencies!" Lonnie Brennan, *Boston Broadside*, April 2, 2017. https://www.bostonbroadside.com/showcase/isolate-medicate-liquidate-how-to-fleece-a-senior/

[2] "Joann Bashinsky Golden Flake Heiress – Her Legacy: Stop Guardianship Abuse," Terri LaPoint, *Real News Spark,* February 16, 2021. https://realnewsspark.com/2021/02/11/joann-bashinsky-golden-flake-heiress-her-legacy-stop-guardianship-abuse/

[3] "Retired Alabama Schoolteacher Forced into Hospice Against Her Will," Terri LaPoint, *Real News Spark*, June 25, 2019. https://realnewsspark.com/2019/06/25/retired-alabama-schoolteacher-forced-into-hospice-against-her-will/

[4] "Massachusetts Senior Citizen and Attorney Medically Kidnapped – Estate Plundered – Represents National Epidemic," *Medical Kidnap* staff, *Medical Kidnap*, May 1, 2017. https://medicalkidnap.com/2017/05/01/massachusetts-senior-citizen-and-attorney-medically-kidnapped-estate-plundered-represents-national-epidemic/

Made in the USA
Columbia, SC
17 June 2024